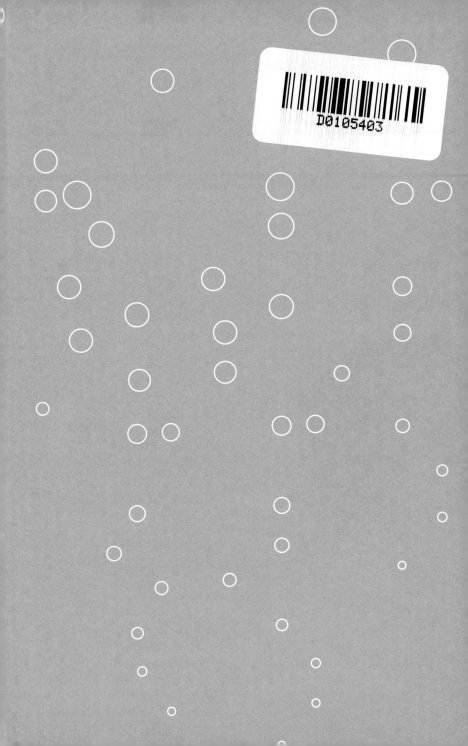

WEDDING SPEECHES

WEDDING
SPEECHES

Perfect Words for a Perfect Day

Agnes Gajewska

NH
NEW
HOLLAND

First published in Australia in 2011 by
New Holland Publishers (Australia) Pty Ltd
Sydney • Auckland • London • Cape Town
www.newholland.com.au

1/66 Gibbes Street Chatswood NSW 2067 Australia
218 Lake Road Northcote Auckland New Zealand
86 Edgware Road London W2 2EA United Kingdom
80 McKenzie Street Cape Town 8001 South Africa

National Library of Australia Cataloguing in Publication data:
Gajewska, Agnes.
Wedding speeches / Agnes Gajewska.
1st ed.
9781742570945 (hbk.)
Includes bibliographical references.
Wedding speeches/Wedding toasts/Wedding ettiquette.
Dewey Number: 808.51

Publisher: Diane Jardine
Publishing manager: Lliane Clarke
Project editor: Rochelle Fernandez
Proofreader: Geraldine Coren
Designer: Celeste Vlok
Production manager: Olga Dementiev
Printer: Toppan Leefung Printing Limited

The author would like to thank:
• *Yale University Press for 'Days' by Karle Wilson Bake*
• *University of Iowa Press for 'Instructions' by Sheri Hostetler*
• *Simon Trowell for 'Cricket Blessing'*
• *Michael Hanrahan for 'Congratulations'*
• *Renu Prasad for 'Straight From the Coach's Mouth'*
All care has been taken to obtain copyright permission for the
pieces used, however please contact the author if there are any
queries.

CONTENTS

INTRODUCTION

Breathe in. Now exhale and repeat 'calm blue ocean'.

You've picked this book up for one of three reasons:

1) You're completely lost and were actually looking for a guide on how to assemble a kayak.

2) You have to speak at a wedding and now you're getting flashbacks to when you spoke at your graduation and fainted.

3) You just asked a friend or family member to speak at your wedding and saw fear pass through their eyes as they accepted.

If it's the former, sorry you're alone on this one. For the latter two, you're in the right spot. *Wedding Speeches* has been designed as a beacon of brilliance and inspiration for wedding speechmakers-to-be. It is here to fill you with confidence and the attitude that'll take you from knee-wobbling shakiness to Martin Luther King brilliance ... or close.

In Section I we cover the basics and give you an insight into becoming the perfect wedding speaker. You'll learn your responsibilities, how to turn a blank sheet of paper into the greatest thing you've ever written, how to fight nerves (and the urge to drink), what to avoid and you'll also be peppered with advice and tips from people in the know.

When you feel the urge to write coming on, you can flick to Section II for sample speeches, toasts and jokes as well as a little help from some of history's greatest literary minds. William Shakespeare, John Donne, John Keats, Henry van Dyke, Victor Hugo and more are waiting to inspire you with more than 200 poems, love letters, quotes, sonnets and expositions.

Breathe in again. There's no need to worry or stress. You were chosen to make a speech because you are important to the bridal couple and not because the fate of the wedding, reception or marriage hangs on your words. So just think of it as your opportunity to tell the people you love just how much they mean to you and how happy you are for them. If you make a few people laugh (or cry) in the process, so be it.

Remember that being asked to speak at a wedding is a great honour; one you should not only embrace, but enjoy.

Section I

FROM STRESSED TO SUCCESSFUL

How to prepare a professional wedding speech

1. ROLES AND RESPONSIBILITIES

Beginnings are difficult. You grab a sheet of paper (or a laptop for the tech-savvy), bring your knowledge of the bridal couple and then sit for hours doodling flowers, hearts and smiley faces. Or checking your email every five minutes. Those first few words are really, really difficult to squeeze out.

Don't fret. There are two sets of good news here. The first is that once you actually start writing, you'll have more of a problem stopping than coming up with material. The second is that you have some guidelines to help you in the form of speakers' roles. These will make it easier for you to write.

TRADITIONAL SPEECHMAKERS
- The master of ceremonies (MC)
- The father of the bride
- The groom
- The best man

If you are one of these lucky people, you will most likely have very defined responsibilities. That is, you will have a list of people to thank, to compliment and to toast as well as implied expectations about what your speech should contain.

The Master Of Ceremonies (MC)

The MC runs the show. You will be the first to speak and it will be your job to ensure that everyone knows what's going on and is having a good time.

Your role is to:

- introduce yourself
- welcome guests and inform them of any customs or games
- prepare guests for the entrance of the bridal party
- introduce bridal party
- one by one, invite each speaker to the microphone
- thank each speaker after their speech
- announce the cutting of the cake
- announce the couple's first dance
- invite the bridal party and/or guests to the dance floor
- invite single ladies for the throwing of the bouquet
- invite single gents for the throwing of the garter
- ask guests to farewell the newlyweds

The Father Of The Bride
Speaking order: First

The father of the bride gets to stir up a few tears by talking about the love for his daughter and welcoming his new son into the family. Make the most of this opportunity—it's not often that grown men can cry in public and be applauded or get their 'dad jokes' laughed at.

Your role is to:
- thank the MC for the introduction
- thank guests for coming—especially if they've come from far
- thank everyone who has contributed to the cost of the wedding
- tell an anecdote/offer wedding advice
- compliment the bride
- welcome new son-in-law (and his parents) into the family
- toast the bride and groom

HINT!   If the mother of the bride/your partner is not speaking, don't forget to include her in your well-wishes and thanks!

TIP!   It's nice to say a few words about your new son-in-law. You could give him a compliment, make a funny observation or offer a short anecdote about how you met or when you first heard about him. It will make his side of the wedding party feel more included.

The Groom
Speaking order: Second

The groom's biggest job is to praise his bride, thank all appropriate parties and set up anticipation for the best man's speech.

Your role is to:
- thank the MC for the introduction
- thank the father of the bride for his toast
- thank any previous speakers
- thank guests for attending and for their gifts
- thank both sets of parents
- compliment the bride
- tell anecdote of how you and the bride met or of how you fell in love
- thank your best man
- thank and toast the bridesmaids

HINT!   Instead of toasting the bridesmaids, you might prefer to toast your new wife.

TIP!   If the bride is not making a speech, make sure to offer your thanks on her behalf as well.

The Best Man
Speaking order: Last

The best man is one of the most vital and generally memorable speakers at the reception and, to a large degree, is also the comic relief. You get to make fun of the groom and tell funny anecdotes, but the best of best men also add some depth to their speeches.

Your role is to:
- thank the MC for the introduction
- thank the groom
- thank any previous speakers
- comment on the bridal couple, particularly the groom
- tell a funny anecdote about the groom
- read out any messages/telegrams from absent friends and relatives
- toast the bride and groom

HINT! If you know the bride well, tell a funny story about her too—but be careful to keep all bride jokes light. If in doubt, leave it out.

TIP! A best man's speech isn't a 21st speech. Keep your stories tactful and balance them out with maturity and genuine well-wishes.

NON-TRADITIONAL SPEECHMAKERS

- The mother of the bride
- The father/mother of the groom
- The bride
- The maid/matron of honour

Not all weddings are traditional, which means that you may find yourself here. That's okay; it just means that your role won't be as clearly defined.

As a non-traditional speaker you might be taking the place of a traditional speaker and assuming their responsibilities (for example the mother of the bride might be speaking instead of the father of the bride). In other instances the bride and groom might want to split particular roles between several people or they may have no specific duties for you in mind. The best thing to do is to ask them for directions.

THE MOTHER OF THE BRIDE
Speaking order: After the father of the bride

The mother of the bride gets to pull a few heartstrings as she recounts her relationship with her daughter and welcomes her new son into the family.

Your role is to:
- thank the MC for the introduction
- thank the father of the bride/previous speaker
- talk about your relationship with the bride/offer an anecdote/advice
- compliment the bride
- welcome the groom and his parents into the family
- toast the bride and groom.

HINT! To inject a bit of humour, you could exploit some of the terrible mother-in-law stereotypes.

THE FATHER/MOTHER OF THE GROOM

Speaking order: After father of the bride/mother of the bride

The father/mother of the groom's speech is similar to that of the father of the bride but has less traditional obligation. It's simply your turn to talk about your son, welcome your new daughter and wish them well.

Your role is to:
- thank the MC for the introduction
- thank the father of the bride/previous speaker
- compliment the bridal couple
- welcome the bride and her parents into the family
- talk about groom/offer an anecdote about the groom
- toast the bride and groom.

HINT! To add some humour to the speech you could talk about the effect the bride has had on the groom—has he become more organised? Cleaner? Lazier? More or less punctual?

THE BRIDE
Speaking order: After the groom

The bride's speech can be whatever you want it to be, but generally it involves many thanks to all parties who helped organise and pay for the wedding as well as a compliment for the groom.

Your role is to:
- thank the MC for the introduction
- thank the groom/previous speaker
- repeat the thanks already given
- thank anyone who hasn't been mentioned by the previous speakers
- thank the groom's parents/accept new role in the family
- offer a short anecdote about the groom or family
- compliment your groom
- toast the wedding guests.

HINT!   You might want to tell the story of how you first met the in-laws and how your dread turned to relief.

The Maid/Matron Of Honour
Speaking order: After the groom/bride

The maid/matron of honour doesn't have too many obligations. Generally you get to have a bit of a laugh at the bride's expense and offer your congratulations.

Your role is to:
- thank the MC for the introduction
- thank the groom/previous speaker
- compliment and thank the bride
- thank the groomsmen/ushers/ bridesmaids
- offer a short anecdote about the bride
- toast the bride and groom.

2. PEN TO PAPER

With your roles set out it's time to get to the task of writing. Easy, right? Wrong! This is the time when paranoia, feelings of inadequacy and writer's block can really set in. But it's also a time when you get to reflect on how much the people you're addressing mean to you ... and a great chance to whip out your sense of humour.

STEP 1: CREATE A PLAN!

Grab a sheet of paper and a pen. Do it now. There is nothing like a good plan and when you're preparing for a wedding speech, it's an absolute necessity.

On your sheet of paper list all of the things that are required from you (if you're unsure of your role, have a look at Chapter I and speak to the bridal couple).

When you create your plan, make sure to leave a decent gap between each point so that you can make notes. Under the point that mentions your own material, leave an extra-large space and divide it in half.

Next, fill in the names of the people you need to thank in the relevant spaces. Your outline should look like this:

Father of the bride — speech outline

Thank MC: John Smith

Thank guests for coming from far:
   Uncle Walter (Alaska)
   Cousin Pierre (France)
   Jahnvi (India)

Thank people who contributed to wedding:
   Sheree and Joel (groom's parents) for beverages
   Joanne (dear friend) for chocolate wedding cake

Anecdote/advice/poem

Compliment the bride
Welcome son-in-law and parents (Sheree and Joel)
Toast bride and groom

This is your basic outline which you will add to step-by-step until your speech is wedding perfect.

STEP 2: PICK YOUR MATERIAL

Aside from heartfelt thankyous and an invitation to drink champagne, your speech will also need to contain some of your own material—a story about the bride and/or groom or some words of advice perhaps?

Your options are only as limited as your imagination:

- anecdotes
- advice
- poetry and prose
- astrology readings
- newspaper clippings
- childhood writings of the bride/groom
- a slideshow of photographs
- songs

Before you make your selection, you have to consider three important things:

1)   Time

Even if you feel your speech is the height of brilliance, chances are that the wedding guests will have to sit through several speeches before or after yours and if you take too long they will fall asleep in their plates. To avoid spaghetti-in-hair situations, keep your speech under 5 minutes.

2)   Balance

The best wedding speeches have a balance of humour and poignancy. Injecting a bit of humour into what you say will make it more enjoyable for the guests. But remember that a wedding speech is not a comedy routine and the couple and guests will want to hear some heartfelt words as well.

3)   *Personality*
The couple chose you because they love you, so keeping your personality in your speech is important. Keep this in mind and select material that you feel comfortable with, not the material that you think a wedding speaker should deliver.

From here you just have to decide which material you want to include in your speech. Since you only have a limited time to speak and won't be able to chronicle the groom's or bride's life from age two, it's best to stick with two pieces of material. Any more might hazard vegetable throwing from the crowd.

Once you've selected two types of material, write them into your wedding speech outline.

STEP 3: RESEARCH
The best speeches, no matter how effortless they may seem, are the product of good research. Put some work into it and you will be rewarded with a look of amused shock and appreciation from the bride and groom. And when you are, it will be satisfying.

Luckily, doing wedding speech research is actually a lot of fun. After all, in most cases it involves reliving funny moments and thinking about what the couple means to you.

Here are a few tips to help you get the most out of each type of material:

For anecdotes:
- Write down as many funny/touching stories about the bride/groom/couple as you can
- Speak to the couple's friends and family to get stories/information/photos
- Speak to the couple's colleagues
- Google their names, check facts, dig out pictures, do what you must

HINT! Be careful to explain every anecdote and ensure that everyone is on the same page with you or at the end you might be laughing alone.

For advice:
- Write down advice from your personal experience.
- Speak to other married people and gather their advice
- Watch a movie or television show that the couple likes and get some ironic marriage advice
- Flick through Chapter Ten in this book
- Have a look online and in other books.

For poetry and prose
- Make a list of your favourite poets/books
- Speak to family, friends and librarians about their favourite poets
- Find out whether the couple has a favourite poet or writer
- Look online
- Read Section II of this book!

For astrology readings
- Find out the couple's zodiac signs
- Search magazines for weekly, quarterly and annual astrology readings
- Look through astrology books

If you're using props/audio-visual equipment
- Collect photographs and music
- Buy props
- Organise everything you need with the venue.

TIP!   Keep a notepad near you whenever possible—you never know when genius will strike.

WHAT NOT TO DO
- Don't insult the bride—it's her special day, don't ruin it for the sake of a joke.
- Don't tell in-jokes.
- Don't criticise the wedding or reception.
- Don't put pressure on the newlyweds to buy a house or have babies.
- Don't mention ex-partners, break-ups or other sensitive subjects.

Go back to your wedding speech outline and write your ideas in each of the columns. It should look something like this:

Anecdote/advice/poem

Anecdote	Poem
Kate got drunk at 2 yrs old	'Our Hearts' – Guy de Maupassant
Kate used to put sandwich bags on her feet to do the moonwalk	'The Owl and the Pussy Cat' – Edward Lear
Kate sleepwalking	'I Love You' – Carl Sandburg
Kate saved baby bird	Tristram – Edwin Arlington Robinson

STEP 4: FINDING A MESSAGE

Every good speech needs a good message to keep it smooth, fluid and interesting. Without one it can become splintered and sound very much like rambling. So you need to work out a common thread that will take you from beginning to end.

You might want to talk about how the bride has always had a sense of adventure and here she is at the beginning of her biggest one or about how the groom has always been particular about the things he loves and the bride is his best choice so far.

What you are looking for is something that will link everything in your speech together and make it sound fluid and complete.

Possible themes:

- dancing
- responsibility
- animals
- punctuality
- adventure
- sense of humour
- selflessness
- weather

Once you've decided on your message, look at your list of possible materials and decide which ones most easily work into it. Cut the list down until you've got one or two left.

STEP 5: BEGINNINGS AND ENDINGS

The beginning of your speech should hook the guests in and make them hang onto your every word, while the ending should offer closure and a chance for them to applaud your efforts. So it's important to start and finish on a strong note.

Tips for writing beginnings:

- Use a funny one-liner or joke to ease the guests in.
- Find a famous quote that sums up your message.
- If you think you're likely to feel nervous on the day, write a joke about it.
- Introduce the theme or message of your speech in your first line.

Tips for writing endings:

- Make a toast—it'll not only recognise the people you are toasting, but also give your speech a finite end
- When you write your toast make sure it's short and easy to repeat
- Poignant poetry works well at the end
- Round off your speech by ending with the message or theme you chose

TIP!   Be emotional! This is your chance to be as soppy as you like. Sentimental stuff that would get you beaten up at work will be applauded by the audience – so long as it is sincere. So express your emotions as much as possible

STEP 6: PUT IT TOGETHER

Congratulations! You've done all of the hard work, now all you have to do is stitch it together. Using your plan as a guide, write out each section until you have a rough speech. Then refine it until you're happy.

STEP 7: FINISHING OFF

When you feel that your speech is perfect, practise timing yourself. Make sure that you speak slowly. From here cut and edit the speech until it is the desired length (between two and five minutes).

Once it's perfect, give yourself a pat on the back and transfer it to palm cards. You can either transfer the entire thing or, if you are going to have time to memorise it, transfer it in point form.

3. USING SOURCE MATERIAL

Sadly we weren't all born with Shakespearean prose flowering out of our mouths, but that doesn't mean that we can't be a little bit poetic when the time calls for it. And it might call for you when you're putting together your wedding speech.

After all, reciting a poem, adding a line from your favourite book, a love letter or even a (very) short story can add a lovely, quirky or sophisticated touch if done properly.

HOW TO PICK SOURCE MATERIAL

When you're making your selection you need to take several things into consideration:

1. The tone of your speech
2. How comfortable you are with the subject matter—don't recite Renaissance poetry if you feel awkward.
3. The message you want to deliver
4. The length—do you want the poem to be a definitive part of your speech or just a piece of wisdom or advice?

With this figured out, select a range of potential source materials and read each one several times, narrowing your selection until you have two or three.

Print each one on a piece of paper and note all the ways in which you can relate each back to the bridal couple or to your message. This should not only give you the tools with which to tie the material into your speech, but an indication as to which of the pieces will best fit in with what you are trying to achieve.

HINT! Don't pick a poem just because it's famous. Make sure it resonates with you or you won't feel it.

WHEN TO USE SOURCE MATERIAL

It's completely up to you where you want to insert the source material. However, there are a few key places where it works well:

1. At the beginning—you can start your speech with a quote, e.g. 'Goethe once said that we are shaped and fashioned by what we love. That's very true. I'd like to thank my beautiful daughter, Rebecca, for my bald head (pause) ... and the smile on my face.'

2. As a segue into another part of your speech, e.g. '...so you see, Debbie, has always been a little stubborn. Knowing this, I'd like to impart some words of wisdom from a poem by Edwin Arlington Robinson to help her in married life:

   I am not one
   Who must have everything; yet I must have
   My dreams if I must live, for they are mine.

Wisdom is not one word and then another,
Till words are like dry leaves under a tree;
Wisdom is like a dawn that comes up slowly
Out of an unknown ocean.

Unexpected things happen and plans change, but as long as the pair of you stubbornly hold onto the most important of your dreams and give way to things that don't matter, you'll find that your marriage will be one of happiness and wisdom ...'

3. At the end—as a strong finish, e.g. 'I will finish my speech with some wise words from Henry van Dyke.
   Time is:
   Too Slow for those who Wait,
   Too Swift for those who Fear,
   Too Long for those who Grieve,
   Too Short for those who Rejoice;
   But for those who Love, Time is eternity.
   Please raise a toast to Andrea and Luke's eternity.'

GOLDEN RULES OF POETRY

Reciting

There is an art to delivering poetry. It isn't easy and if you are going to include a poem in your piece you should practise, practise, practise.

Some things to remember:

1. Poetry is like acting, you need to put emotion into your voice
2. Pronunciation—make sure you have it right

3. Don't rush through it
4. Enunciate—you need to speak clearly
5. You have to commit; poems will be at their most effective if you give it all you've got.
6. Try to learn the poem, it'll come out more naturally
7. Understand what you're saying or it won't sound genuine
8. Do not. Put breaks where. they are not. needed. When reading poetry recite each sentence, not each line.
9. Be vocal—even if you have a microphone, whispering is no good
10. Plan pauses and words to emphasise for effect
11. If you forget where you are don't stop or apologise, just take a breath and start from where you left off
12. Some poems require different voices; be mindful of this

HINT! Record yourself reciting the poem. Try to do it in the bathroom. Your voice will echo more in there so there'll be no getting away from it.

GETTING IT RIGHT

Poetry isn't something that we hear a lot of, so here are a couple of games you can play with a friend or tape recorder to ensure that you get the most out of it.

Game 1—Emphasis

Print your poem out and highlight four key words in each stanza. Read each stanza four times, each time placing the emphasis on a different highlighted word. Listen to how the meaning of the poem changes. Ask your friend which way sounds best or listen to your recording and note which you like best.

Game 2—Speed

Read your poem slowly—much slower than you were planning to—leaving pauses in between stanzas and after strong sentences. Then read it again as fast as you can. Record both attempts and listen to the difference or get your friend to do this exercise while you listen to the difference as an audience member.

Game 3—Voices

For poems with more than one voice, highlight each voice in a different colour then assign a character to each. For example, green for your grandmother, yellow for your cat, blue for your boss and so forth. Read the poem using the prescribed voices. Make sure to record yourself and listen to the effect. Work on finding the right voices for your poem.

4. THE PERFECT DELIVERY

Let's get one thing out of the way—public speaking doesn't come naturally to most people. A famous study found that the fear of public speaking ranks higher in most people's minds than the fear of death, fear of spiders and fear of heights. So, in other words, it's perfectly normal to be nervous about your wedding speech.

Ready for the good news? There are some fantastic methods that can help you fight the jitters.

STRAIGHT FROM THE COACH'S MOUTH

Three basic tips on overcoming your public speaking fear:

1)   *Remember that nerves are a normal part of public speaking*

Feeling nervous is a completely normal part of the speaking experience. You'll feel some anxiety prior to your speech and this may continue during the speech itself. Don't feel ashamed or feel that you are failing at your task simply because you are nervous. The truth is that all speakers experience nerves, but the audience rarely notices. Stay strong and remember that you can get through your speech if you give yourself a chance!

2)   *Prepare your speech*

If you were a musician you wouldn't play a concert without rehearsing first. The same goes for public speaking. It's fine to spend hours editing a speech on your computer, but preparation that really counts is vocal rehearsal. Quite simply that means practising your speech out loud, whether it's in front of a small group of friends, alone or even with a pet! This is the only way to gain the requisite familiarity with the material.

3)   *Remember to breathe*

Okay, this sounds a bit obvious. But breathing is a very common problem for first-time public speakers. The heart is racing and the adrenaline is rising, so quite naturally there is a tendency to speak fast too. The problem is that it's hard to breathe normally if you're gabbling through your speech at a hundred miles an hour—not to mention the problems the audience will have keeping up with you. So try to remember to use your breathing to moderate the pace of your delivery. Make a mental note to periodically stop, pause, take a deep breath and then continue—you'll feel a lot calmer.

– Renu Prasad, Public speaking coach

KEEP OFF THE CHAMPERS

Although gaining a little Dutch courage by drinking might seem like a good idea, it can turn on you. Alcohol can make you more prone to slurring, going off on tangents, including material that was not previously in your speech (and possibly for good reason) and shouting out things like I LOVE YOU. YOU'RE NICE. So keep it to one and stay sober.

HINT!   Before you start make sure the room is ready for you to speak — wait until everyone's finished clapping.

EYE CONTACT

Grab some nerves, mix them in with a room of wedding guests and the safety of your speech on a piece of paper and chances are that you'll spend most of your time looking at your notes and not at the audience.

Try to avoid this. You can either prepare cue cards, which will give you time to look up, or write (LOOK UP!) and (PAUSE) in your speech to remind yourself.

TIP!   Focus on one person in the room for every 20 seconds of your speech. Pretend you're just having a chat with them.

JOKES

Jokes are all about the delivery, so don't be afraid to laugh. People will be looking to you for response cues, so a chuckle can be helpful. Just make sure you deliver the punchline first and moderate yourself. Laughing too long at your own joke won't leave the best impression.

HINT!   If your joke dies, don't panic or run off stage in a sob — work
         past it. If you feel confident you can even say something like,
         'Sorry, that was much funnier when I wrote it' or, 'My cat/
         dog found that one hilarious'...and move on.

SMILE!

Even if your knees are shaking hard, don't let it show on your face. Smile and look happy. People will trust it if you do a convincing job.

HINT!   If the nerves are tensing up your face, think of some happy
         memories before you deliver your speech.

FAKE IT TILL YOU MAKE IT

If public speaking makes you nervous, you will be nervous. So the best idea is to fake it till you make it. If you pretend you're confident and speak with bravado the guests will believe you.

HINT!   Remember that the guests are on your side. They want to
         see you do well, they want to hear nice stories, they want
         to laugh, they are very glad it's you and not them doing the
         speech and they will most likely be drinking.

WHAT NOT TO DO

- Wing it—always be prepared. Always!
- Make it long—you'll send the guests to sleep
- Try to be something you're not. If you're not a comedian, keep the jokes to a minimum; if you're not a romantic, don't spout Shakespearean sonnets.
- Ramble or mumble

TIP! Write out some of these hints on spare cue cards and take them along for moral support and motivation.

A GOOD ENDING

Be kind to the people, especially to the ones who are drunk or weren't listening, and finish your speech with a definitive ending. That way they'll know to either clap or toast.

5. THE END OF THE BEGINNING

We've come to the end of Part I and this is where the real fun begins. But before you move onto the source material and run away with your speech writing skills, let's look over a quick checklist:

Before writing a speech:
- find out your role—who you have to thank
- find out the order of speakers

Writing a speech:
- create a plan
- pick two types of material
- research
- find a message
- write the beginning and end
- put it together
- Finish off by polishing and timing yourself

If you'd like to use poetry:
- pick material that suits your speech
- decide which part of your speech you'd like to include it in
- learn to recite it
- practise, practise, practise

Delivering the speech
- remember nerves are normal
- practise
- breathe
- don't drink
- keep eye contact
- laugh with the audience
- fake it till you make it
- finish on a toast

Most importantly, remember to have fun. You were chosen to speak because you are you. Nobody less. Draw confidence from that and enjoy yourself.

Good luck! You'll be great!

Section II

WORDS TO
INSPIRE YOU

A QUICK NOTE FROM THE AUTHOR

Organising source material is a bit like doing the bridal waltz. Although it looks smooth in the end, a few things are bound to overlap, a few things are missed or forgotten in the glory of the moment and some quirky additions are made.

As you will notice, rather than by speaker, the source part of this book is divided by theme so you can find what you're looking for. We hope this book brings you lots of inspiration.

6. SHORT AND SWEET

POIGNANT

I like not only to be loved but also to be told that I am loved. The realm of silence is large enough beyond the grave. This is the world of light and speech. And I shall take leave to tell you that you are very dear.

George Eliot

———⇒•⇐———

On the banks of the James River, a husband erected a tombstone in memory of his wife, one of those 100 maidens who had come to Virginia in 1619 to marry the lonely settlers. The stone bore this legend: 'She touched the soil of Virginia with her little foot and the wilderness became a home'.

Eudora Ramsay Richardson

———⇒•⇐———

To love someone deeply gives you strength. Being loved by someone deeply gives you courage.

Lao Tzu

Love is a canvas furnished by nature and embroidered by imagination.

Voltaire

I love thee with the breath, smiles, tears, of all my life!

Elizabeth Barrett Browning

A house without a woman and firelight is like a body without soul or spirit.

Benjamin Franklin

Whatever our souls are made of, his and mine are the same.

Emily Brontë

There is no more lovely, friendly and charming relationship, communion or company than a good marriage.

Martin Luther

We are the perfect example of the whole being greater than its parts. Alone, I am lost. With you, I feel I can achieve a life that is peaceful and caring and filled with laughter.

Marion C. Garretty

———❖———

We never live so intensely as when we love strongly. We never realise ourselves so vividly as when we are in full glow of love for others.

Walter Rauschenbusch

———❖———

It is a glorious privilege to live, to know, to act, to listen, to behold, to love. To look up at the blue summer sky; to see the sun sink slowly beyond the line of the horizon; to watch the worlds come twinkling into view, first one by one, and the myriads that no man can count, and lo! the universe is white with them; and you and I are here.

Marco Morrow

———❖———

For, you see, each day I love you more, today more than yesterday and less than tomorrow.

Rosemonde Gerard

———❖———

Life has taught us that love does not consist in gazing at each other but in looking outward together in the same direction.

Antoine de Saint-Exupery

———❖———

No one knows our secret. We seem such an ordinary couple. How could they know the depth and wonder of our love?

Brian E. Williams

One man by himself is nothing. Two people who belong together make a world.

Hans Margolius

The entire sum of existence is the magic of being needed by just one person.

Vi Putnam

Now we will feel no rain, for each of us will be shelter for the other. Now we will feel no cold, for each of us will be warmth for the other. Now there is no more loneliness, for each of us will be companion to the other. There is only one life before us and our seasons will be long and good.

From an Apache wedding blessing

The two most beautiful things in the universe are the starry heavens above our heads, and the feeling of duty in our hearts.

Jacques-Bénigne Bossuet

They gave each other a smile with a future in it.

Ring Lardner

———⟫•⟪———

A NEW LIFE

In the opinion of the world, marriage ends all, as it does in a comedy. The truth is precisely the opposite: it begins all.

Anne Sophie Swetchine

———⟫•⟪———

ADVICE

Between husband and wife there should be no question as to meum and tuum. All things should be in common between them, without any distinction or means of distinguishing.

Martin Luther

———⟫•⟪———

There are only two times in a man's life when he can't understand a woman—before marriage and after marriage.

Anonymous

———⟫•⟪———

There is a place you can touch a woman that will drive her crazy. Her heart.

Melanie Griffith

———⟫•⟪———

'Life is always flowing on like a river sometimes with murmurs, sometimes without bending this way and that, we do not exactly see why; now in beautiful picturesque places, now through barren and uninteresting scenes, but always flowing with a look of treachery about it; it is so swift, so voiceless, yet so continuous.

Frederick William Faber

⸻

Keep your eyes wide open before the wedding, half shut afterwards.

Benjamin Franklin

⸻

The average woman would rather have beauty than brains, because the average man can see better than he can think.

Anonymous

By all means marry; if you get a good wife, you'll be happy. If you get a bad one, you'll become a philosopher.

Socrates

⸻

Don't marry for money, you can borrow it cheaper.

Scottish proverb

⸻

A good wife always forgives her husband when she's wrong.

Milton Berle

⸻

UPS AND DOWNS

An occasional lucky guess as to what makes a wife tick is the best a man can hope for. Even then, no sooner has he learned how to cope with the tick than she tocks.

Ogden Nash

The two secrets to a long-lasting and happy marriage: have a good sense of humour and a short memory.

Anonymous

Let me give you the same advice my father gave me upon the occasion of my own wedding: there are two ways to handle a woman, and no one knows either of them.

Anonymous

FUNNY

With her marriage she got a new name and a dress (address).

Anonymous

I think men who have a pierced ear are better prepared for marriage. They've experienced pain and bought jewellery.

Rita Rudner

Do you take this man ... this woman...to be your lawful wedded ... from this day forth, to have and to hold, forsaking all others, for richer for poorer, in sickness and in health ... till death us do part. It's a pretty tall order. No employer would dare to demand such a contract. It's tantamount to slavery. Pass me the papers. I'll renew my subscription.

Richard Alan

It has been said it is impossible to love and be wise. But for you I can't help but to love.

Francis Bacon

There are terrible temptations which it requires strength and courage to yield to.

Oscar Wilde

He let her know who was boss early on. He looked her right in the eye and clearly said, 'You're the boss.'

Anonymous

Marriage sets mathematics on its head—for at one swoop it halves all troubles. Being shared, multiplies joys out of all reckoning, divides responsibilities, doubles perception.

Pam Brown

Don't take life too seriously; you'll never get out of it alive.

Elbert Hubbard

———»·o·«———

I require only three things of a man. He must be handsome, ruthless and stupid.

Dorothy Parker

———»·o·«———

Marriage means commitment. Of course, so does insanity.

Anonymous

———»·o·«———

It's not whether you win or lose, but how you place the blame.

Anonymous

———»·o·«———

I love being married. It's so great to find that one special person you want to annoy for the rest of your life.

Rita Rudner

———»·o·«———

I know that marriage is a legal and religious alliance entered into by a man who can't sleep with the window shut and a woman who can't sleep with the window open.

Ogden Nash (from I do, I will, I have)

———»·o·«———

Behind every great man there is a surprised woman.

Maryon Pearson

Most girls seem to marry men who happen to be like their fathers. Maybe that's why so many mothers cry at weddings!

Jenny Éclair

To keep your marriage brimming,
with love in the loving cup—
whenever you're wrong, admit it,
whenever you're right, shut up.

Ogden Nash (from Marriage Lines)

Now some people think it's jolly for to lead
a single life,
But I believe in marriage and the
comforts of a wife.
In fact you might have quarrels, just an odd one
now and then,
It's worth your while a-falling out to
make it up again.

English folk song

The marriage state, with the affection suitable to it, is the completest image of heaven and hell we are capable of receiving in this life.

Richard Steele

———❖———

They say when a man holds a woman's hand before marriage it is love; after marriage it is self-defence.

Anonymous

———❖———

WISDOM

If I had my life to live over ... I would perhaps have more actual troubles, but I'd have fewer imaginary ones.

Nadine Stair

———❖———

Anyone can carry his burden,
however hard, until nightfall.
Anyone can do his work,
however hard, for one day.
Anyone can live sweetly,
patiently, lovingly, purely, till
the sun goes down. And this is
all that life really means.

Robert Louis Stevenson

———❖———

Love is friendship set to music.

Anonymous

—————≫•≪—————

Marriage is like wine—it gets better with age.

Dudley Moore

—————≫•≪—————

Marriage is popular because it combines the maximum of temptation with the maximum of opportunity.

George Bernard Shaw

—————≫•≪—————

Life is either a daring adventure or nothing.

Helen Keller

—————≫•≪—————

A toast to sweethearts—may all sweethearts become married couples and may all married couples remain sweethearts.

Unknown

—————≫•≪—————

Enjoy the little things,
for one day you may
look back and discover
they were the big things.

Author unknown

—————≫•≪—————

Ever wonder why God gives us two? A right hand to show the left what to do. One ear to listen and one to hear the problems of others, their laughter and fears. One eye to watch and one to behold the beautiful treasures that life has to hold. One foot to travel and one to stand tall. Two feet to land on if we should fall. One man to stand by a woman's side; one woman to cherish being his bride. The love between partners comes shining through, and that is the reason God has made two.

Author unknown

———⊷◦⊶———

When love reigns, the impossible may be attained.

Indian proverb

———⊷◦⊶———

May your love be like the misty rain, gentle coming in but flooding the river.

African proverb

———⊷◦⊶———

Married couples who love each other tell each other a thousand things without talking.

Chinese proverb

———⊷◦⊶———

The happiest people in life don't have the best of everything, they make the best of everything they have.

Unknown

———⊷◦⊶———

We are shaped and fashioned by what we love.

Johann Wolfgang von Goethe

———◆———

And think not you can guide the course of love. For love, if it finds you worthy, shall guide your course.

Kahlil Gibran

———◆———

If the day and the night are such that you greet them with joy, and life emits a fragrance like flowers and sweet-scented herbs, is more elastic, more starry, more immortal—that is your success.

Henry David Thoreau

———◆———

You may paddle all day long, but it is when you come back at nightfall, and look in the familiar room, that you find Love or Death awaiting you beside the stove; and the most beautiful adventures are not those we go to seek.

Robert Louis Stevenson

———◆———

A marriage makes of two fractional lines a whole; it gives to two purposeless lives a work, and doubles the strength of each to perform it; it gives to two questioning natures a reason for living, and something to live for.

Mark Twain

———◆———

May heaven grant you in all things you heart's desire—
husband, house and a happy peaceful home. For there is
nothing better in this world than that a man and a woman,
sharing the same ideas, keep house together. It discomforts
their enemies and makes the hearts of their friends glad—but
they themselves know more about it than anyone.

Homer (from The Odyssey*)*

To love is nothing. To be loved is something. To love, and be
loved, is everything.

T. Tolis

Love, the magician, knows this little trick whereby two people
walk in different directions yet always remain side by side.

Hugh Prather

A successful marriage is not a gift; it is an achievement.

Ann Landers

Love is that condition in which the happiness of another
person is essential to your own.

Robert Heinlein

Every enduring marriage involves an unconditional commitment to an imperfect person.

Gary Smalley

———»‹‹———

The great secret of a successful marriage is to treat all disasters as incidents and none of the incidents as disasters.

Harold Nicholson

———»‹‹———

A happy marriage is a long conversation that always seems too short.

Andre Maurois

———»‹‹———

SPEECH JOKES

It's not as great a day for the bride as she thinks, she's not marrying the best man.

———»‹‹———

To the bride: please put your hand on the table. To the groom: Now please lay your hand on top of your bride's. Very good. I want everyone to witness this touching moment. (GROOM), I also want you to enjoy it ... because it's the last time you'll ever have the upper hand.

———»‹‹———

May the happy couple lie, steal and cheat—May they lie in each other's arms, may they steal away for a blissful honeymoon and may they cheat time to live as long as possible.

———————

The brain is a wonderful thing. It never stops functioning from the time you're born until the moment you stand up to make a speech.

Herbert V Prochnow and Herbert V Prochnow Jr

———————

The trouble with being the best man at a wedding is that you never get to prove it.

———————

I can honestly say that in all the years I've known him, no one has ever questioned (GROOM)'s intelligence. In fact, I've never heard anyone even mention it.

———————

If I could say a few words ... I'd be a better public speaker.

———————

On the night before the wedding I asked the groom what he wanted to get from his marriage. He said 'Well, I want to be a model husband. I want to be a model citizen. And I want to be a model lover!' Being a naïve chap, I looked up 'model' in the dictionary. It said 'A small miniature replica of the real thing!'

———————

To the bride and groom—may all their ups and downs be between the sheets!

I'd like to thank you for your presence and thank you for your presents.

Steve Harris

Now, before I start, the hotel management has asked me to request that, for reasons of health and safety none of you get up on top of the chairs and tables during my standing ovation.

Ladies and gentlemen, I'd like to thank all of you for being here today, especially since many of you knew that I'd want to say a few words ... it's very touching that you still decided to come.

Thanks, Dad, for the kind words. I hope $20 was enough.

Some of you might be feeling nervous, anxious and more than a little uncomfortable. If you are, you've probably just married (GROOM).

Attractive, funny, charming ... but enough about me ...

———>•<———

They say the best speeches are short and to the point, so thank you and goodnight!

———>•<———

I've been told that should I ever get nervous, I should just imagine everyone in their underwear. So may I compliment the bridal couple on their matching G-strings.

———>•<———

7. ROMANTIC

Being your slave what should I do but tend,
Upon the hours and times of your desire?
I have no precious time at all to spend;
Nor services to do, till you require.
Nor dare I chide the world-without-end hour,
Whilst I (my sovereign) watch the clock for you,
Nor think the bitterness of absence sour,
When you have bid your servant once adieu.
Nor dare I question with my jealous thought,
Where you may be, or your affairs suppose.
But like a sad slave stay and think of nought
Save, where you are, how happy you make those,
So true a fool is love that in your Will,
Though you do any thing he thinks no ill.

William Shakespeare, Being Your Slave
(Sonnet LVII)

TIP! If you're having a bit of trouble with poems written in old English, have a look for a break-down of the poem online or in a writing guide.

O Mistress mine, where are you roaming?
O! stay and hear; your true love's coming.
That can sing both high and low.
Trip no further, pretty sweeting;
Journeys end in lovers meeting,
Every wise man's son doth know.
What is love? 'Tis not hereafter;
Present mirth hath present laughter;
What's to come is still unsure.
In delay there lies no plenty;
Then come kiss me, sweet and twenty;
Youth's a stuff will not endure.

William Shakespeare, Feste's Song

It's all I have to bring to-day
This, and my heart beside,
This, and my heart, and all the fields,
And all the meadows wide.
Be sure you count, should I forget,
Some one the sun could tell,
This, and my heart, and all the bees
Which in the clover dwell.

Emily Dickinson, It's all I Have to Bring Today

Come live with me, and be my love,
And we will some new pleasures prove
Of golden sands, and christall brookes,
With silken lines, and silver hookes.

There will the river whispering runne
Warm'd by the eyes, more than the Sunne.
And there the 'inamor'd fish will stay,
Begging themselves they may betray.

When thou wilt swimme in that live bath,
Each fish, which every channel hath,
Will amourously to thee swimme,
Gladder to catch thee, than thou him.

If thou, to be so seene, beest loath,
By Sunne, or Moone, thou darknest both,
And if my selfe have leave to see,
I need not their light, having thee.

Let others freenze with angling reeds,
And cut their legges, with shells and weeds,
Or treacherously poore fish beset,
With strangling snare, or windowie net:

Let coarse bold hands, from slimy nest
The bedded fish in banks out-west,
Or curious traitors, sleavesilke flies
Bewitch poore fishes wandring eyes.
For thee, thou needst no such deceit,

For thou thy selfe art thine owne bait;
That fish, that is not catch'd thereby,
Alas, is wiser farre than I.

John Donne, The Baite

———➤◦◄———

I wonder by my troth, what thou, and I
Did, till we lov'd? Were we not wean'd till then?
But suck'd on country pleasures, childishly?
Or snorted we in the seaven sleepers den?
T'was so; But this, all pleasures fancies bee.
If ever any beauty I did see,
Which I desir'd, and got, t'was but a dreame of thee.

And now good morrow to our waking soules,
Which watch not one another out of feare;
For love, all love of other sights controules,
And makes one little roome, an every where.
Let sea-discoverers to new worlds have gone,
Let Maps to other, worlds on worlds have showne,
Let us possesse one world each hath one, and is one.

My face in thine eye, thine in mine appears,
And true plaine hearts doe in the faces rest,
Where can we finde two better hemispheares
Without sharpe North, without declining West?
What ever dyes, was not mixt equally:
If our two loves be one, or, thou and I
Love so alike, that none doe slacken, none can die.

John Donne, The Good-Morrow

Come live with me and be my love,
And we will all the pleasures prove,
That hills and valleys, dales and fields,
And all the craggy mountains yields.

There we will sit upon the rocks,
And see the shepherds feed their flocks,
By shallow rivers to whose falls
Melodious birds sings madrigals.

And I will make thee beds of roses
With a thousand fragrant posies,
A cap of flowers, and a kirtle
Embroidered all with leaves of myrtle;

A gown made of the finest wool
Which from our pretty lambs we pull;
Fair lined slippers for the cold,
With buckles of the purest gold;

A belt of straw and ivy buds,
With Coral clasps and amber studs:
And if these pleasures may thee move,
Come lie with me and be my love.

The shepherds' swains shall dance and sing
For thy delight each May morning:
If these delights thy mind may move,
Then live with me and be my love.

Christopher Marlowe,
The Passionate Shepherd to his Love

HINT!   Although a poem may sound magical in its entirety, you
        may not have the time to recite the whole thing. Have a
        look at each stanza—you'll find that each one will have a
        lot of depth and meaning and many can stand alone.

I wonder do you feel to-day
As I have felt since, hand in hand,
We sat down on the grass, to stray
In spirit better through the land,
This morn of Rome and May?

For me, I touched a thought, I know,
Has tantalized me many times,
(Like turns of thread the spiders throw
Mocking across our path) for rhymes
To catch at and let go.

Help me to hold it: first it left
The yellowing fennel, run to seed
There, branching from the brickwork's cleft,
Some old tomb's ruin: yonder weed
Took up the floating weft,

Where one small orange cup amassed
Five beetles,blind and green they grope
Among the honey'meal,-and last,
Everywhere on the grassy slope
I traced it. Hold it fast!

The champaign with its endless fleece
Of feathery grasses everywhere!
Silence and passion, joy and peace,
An everlasting wash of air—
Rome's ghost since her decease.

Such life here, through such lengths of hours,
Such miracles performed in play,
Such primal naked forms of flowers,
Such letting Nature have her way
While Heaven looks from its towers.

How say you? Let us, O my dove,
Let us be unashamed of soul,
As earth lies bare to heaven above.
How is it under our control
To love or not to love?

I would that you were all to me,
You that are just so much, no more—
Nor yours, nor mine—nor slave nor free!
Where does the fault lie? what the core
Of the wound, since wound must be?

I would I could adopt your will,
See with your eyes, and set my heart
Beating by yours, and drink my fill
At your soul's springs—your part, my part
In life, for good and ill.

No. I yearn upward-touch you close,
Then stand away. I kiss your cheek,
Catch your soul's warmth—I pluck the rose
And love it more than tongue can speak
Then the good minute goes.

Already how am I so far
Out of that minute? Must I go
Still like the thistle-ball, no bar,
Onward, whenever light winds blow,
Fixed by no friendly stay?

Just when I seemed about to learn!
Where is the thread now? Off again!
The old trick! Only I discern-
Infinite passion, and the pain
Of finite hearts that yearn.

Robert Browning Two in the Campagna

Not from the whole wide world I chose thee,
Sweetheart, light of the land and the sea!
The wide, wide world could not inclose thee,
For thou art the whole wide world to me.

Richard Watson Gilder

When Love with unconfined wings
Hovers within my Gates;
And my divine Althea brings
To whisper at the Grates:
When I lye tangled in her haire,
And fetter'd to her eye;
The Birds, that wanton in the Aire,
Know no such Liberty.

When flowing Cups run swiftly round.
With no allaying Thames,
Our carelesse heads with Roses bound,
Our hearts with Loyall Flames;
When thirsty griefe in Wine we steepe,
When Healths are draughts go free,
Fishes that tipple in the Deepe,
Know no such Libertie.

When (like committed Linnets) I
With shriller throat shall sing
The sweetness, Mercy, Majesty,
And glories of my King;
When I shall voice aloud, how Good
He is, How Great should be;
Inlarged Winds that curle the Flood,
Know no such Liberty.

Stone Walls do not a Prison make,
Nor Iron bars a Cage;
Mindes innocent and quiet take

That for an Hermitage;
If I have freedome in my Love,
And in my soule am free;
Angels alone that soar above,
Injoy such Liberty.

Richard Lovelace, To Althea from Prison

All the breath and the bloom of the year in the bag of one
bee: All the wonder and wealth of the mine in the heart of
one gem: In the core of one pearl all the shade and the shine
of the sea: Breath and bloom, shade and shine,
wonder, wealth, and—how far above them—
Truth, that's brighter than gem,
Trust, that's purer than pearl,
Brightest truth, purest trust in the universe—all were for me
In the kiss of one girl.

Robert Browning Summum Bonum

Ay! though the gorgèd asp of passion feed
On my boy's heart, yet have I burst the bars,
Stood face to face with Beauty, known indeed
The Love which moves the Sun and all the stars!

Oscar Wilde, from *Apologia*

If yet I have not all thy love,
Deare, I shall never have it all,
I cannot breathe one other sigh, to move,
Nor can intreat one other teare to fall,
And all my treasure, which should purchase thee,
Sighs, teares, and oaths, and letters I have spent.
Yet no more can be due to mee,
Than at the bargaine made was ment,
If then thy gift of love were partiall,
That some to mee, some should to others fall,
Deare, I shall never have Thee All.

Or if then though gavest mee all,
All was but All, which thou hadst then;
But if in thy heart, since, there be or shall,
New love created bee, by other men,
Which have their stocks intire, and can in teares,
In sighs, in oaths, and letters outbid mee,
This new love may beget new feares,
For, this love was not vowed by thee.
And yet it was, thy gift being generall,
The ground, thy heart is mine, what ever shall
Grow there, deare, I should have it all.

Yet I would not have all yet,
Hee that hath all can have no more,
And since my love doth every day admit
New growth, thou shouldst have new rewards in store;
Thou canst not every day give me thy heart,
If thou canst give it, then thou never gavest it:

Love's riddles are, that tough thy heart depart;
It stayes at home, and thou with losing savest it:
But wee will have a way more liberall,
Than changing hearts, to joyne them, so wee shall
Be one, and one anothers All.

John Donne Lovers Infinitenesse

HINT! To get the most out of poetry look deeper than just the literal level. Use your imagination and try to understand whether there are any symbolic messages hidden in the verses.

Time flies,
Suns rise
And shadows fall.
Let time go by.
Love is forever over all.

From an old sun dial

He is the half-part of a blessed man,
Left to be finished by such as she;
And she a fair divided excellence,
Whose fullness of perfection lies in him.

William Shakespeare, The Half-Part of a Blessed
Man, *from* King John)

Strange—to grow up and not be different,
Not beautiful or even very wise ...
o winging-out the way of butterflies,
No sudden blindfold-lifting from the eyes.
Strange—to grow up and still be wondering,
Reverent at petals and snow,
Still holding breath,
Still often tiptoe,
Questioning dew and stars,
Wanting to know!

Mildred Bowers Armstrong, Strange

My heart is like a singing bird
Whose nest is in a watered shoot;
My heart is like an apple tree
Whose boughs are bent with thickset fruit;
My heart is like a rainbow shell
That paddles in a halcyon sea;
My heart is gladder than all these,
Because my love is come to me.

Raise me a dais of silk and down;
Hang it with vair and purple dyes
Carve it in doves and pomegranates,
and peacocks with a hundred eyes;
Work it in gold and silver grapes,
In leaves and silver fleur-de-lys;
Because the birthday of my life
Is come, my love is come to me.

Christina Georgina Rossetti, A Birthday

Had I the heavens' embroidered cloths,
Enwrought with golden and silver light,
The blue and the dim and the dark cloths
Of night and light and the half-light,
I would spread the cloths under your feet:
But I, being poor, have only my dreams;
I have spread my dreams under your feet;
Tread softly because you tread on my dreams.

W.B. Yeats, He Wishes for the Clothes of Heaven

The Fountains mingle with the River
And the Rivers with the Ocean,
The winds of Heaven mix for ever
With a sweet emotion;
Nothing in the world is single;
All things but a law divine
I none spirit meet and mingle.
Why not I with thine?

See the mountains kiss high heaven
And the waves clasp one another;
No sister-flower would be forgiven
If it disdained its brother,
And the sunlight clasps the earth
and the moonbeams kiss the sea:
What are all these kissings worth
If thou kiss not me?

Percy Bysshe Shelley, Love's Philosophy

Who is in love with loveliness,
Need not shake with cold;
For he may tear a star in two,
And frock himself in gold.

Who holds her first within his heart,
In certain favor goes;
If his roof tumbles, he may find
Harbor in a rose.

Lizette Woodworth Reese, Miracle

HINT!   The above poem, 'Miracle', by Lizette Woodworth Reese
could be used to reflect what a lucky (and carefree) lad
the groom is for being able to fall for someone as lovely as
the bride.

O fair! O sweet! when I do look on thee,
In whom all joys so well agree,
Heart and soul do sing in me,
Just accord all music makes;
In thee just accord excelleth,
Where each part in such peace dwelleth,
One of the other beauty takes,
Since, then, truth to all mind telleth
That in thee lives harmony.
Heart and soul do sing in me.

Sir Philip Sidney, O Fair! O Sweet

Glad that I live am I;
That the sky is blue;
Glad for the country lanes,
And the fall of dew.

After the sun the rain,
After the rain the sun;
This is the way of life,
Till the work be done.

All that we need to do,
Be we low or high
Is to see that we grow
Nearer the sky.

Lizette Woodworth Reese, A Little Song of Life

How I loved
Witness, ye days and nights, and all ye hours,
That danced away with down upon your feet,
As all your business were to count my passion!
One day passed by, and nothing saw but love;
Another came, and still 'twas only love:
The suns were wearied out with looking on,
And I untired with loving.
I saw you every day, and all the day;
And every day was still but as the first,
So eager was I still to see you more ...

John Dryden (from All for Love)

Bright star, would I were stedfast as thou art–
Not in lone splendour hung aloft the night
And watching, with eternal lids apart,
Like nature's patient, sleepless Eremite,
The moving waters at their priestlike task
Of pure ablution round earth's human shores,
Or gazing on the new soft-fallen mask
Of snow upon the mountains and the moors–
No–yet still stedfast, still unchangeable,
Pillow'd upon my fair love's ripening breast,
To feel for ever its soft fall and swell,
Awake for ever in a sweet unrest,
Still, still to hear her tender-taken breath,
And so live ever–or else swoon to death.

John Keats, Bright Star Would I Were
Steadfast As Thou Art

———⇒•⇐———

Although I conquer all the earth,
yet for me there is only one city,
In that city there is for me only one house;
And in that house, one room only;
And in that room, a bed.
And one woman sleeps there,
The shining joy and jewel of all my kingdom.

Sanskrit (Author unknown), Although I Conquer

———⇒•⇐———

Man and woman are like the earth,
that brings forth flowers
in summer, and love, but underneath is rock.
Older than flowers, older than ferns, older than
foraminiferae
older than plasm altogether is the soul of a man
underneath.

And when, throughout all the wild orgasms of love
slowly a gem forms, in the ancient, once-more-molten
rocks of two human hearts, two ancient rocks, a man's heart
and a woman's,
that is the crystal of peace, the slow hard jewel
of trust,
the sapphire of fidelity.
The gem of mutual peace emerging from the
wild chaos of love.

D.H. Lawrence (from Fidelity*)*

8. QUIRKY

And what is Love? It is a doll, dressed up
For idleness to cosset, nurse and dandle;
A thing of soft misnomers, so divine
That silly youth doth think to make itself
Divine by loving, and so goes on
Yawning and doting a whole summer long,
Till Miss's comb is made a pearl tiara,
And common Wellingtons turn Romeo boots;
Then Cleopatra lives at number seven,
And Antony resides in Brunswick Square.
Fools! If some passions high have warmed the world,
If Queens and Soldiers have played deep for hearts,
It is no reason why such agonies
Should be more common than the growth of weeds.
Fools! Make me a whole again that weighty pearls
The Queen of Egypt melted, and I'll say
That ye may love in spite of beaver hats.

John Keats, A Modern Love

Take heed of loving mee,
At least remember, I forbade it thee;
Not that I shall repaire my'unthrifty wast.
Of Breath and Blood, upon thy sighes, and teares,
By being to thee then what to me thou wast;
By, so great Joy, our life at once outwears,
Then, lest thy love, by my death, frustrate bee,
If thou love mee, take heed of loving mee.

Take heed of hating mee,
Or too much triumph in the Victorie.
Not that I shall be mine owne officer,
And hate with hate againe retaliate;
But thou wilt lose the stile of conquerour,
If I, thy conquest, perish by the hate.
Then, lest my being nothing lessen thee,
If thou hate mee, take heed of hating mee.

Yet, love and hate mee too,
So, these extreames shall neither office doe;
Love mee, that I may die the gentler way;
Hate mee, because thy love is too great for mee;
Or let these two, themselves, not me, decay;
So shall I, live, thy Stage, not triumph bee;
Lest thou thy love and hate and mee undoe,
To let mee live, O love and hate mee too.

John Donne, The Prohibition

Yet for all this, amongst so many irksome, absurd, troublesome symptoms, inconveniences, phantastical fits and passions which are usually incident to such persons, there be some good and graceful qualities in lovers, which this affection causeth. 'As it makes wise men fools, so many times it makes fools become wise; it makes base fellows become generous, cowards courageous,' as Cardan notes out of Plutarch; covetous, liberal and magnificent; clowns, civil; cruel, gentle; wicked profane persons to become religious; slovens, neat; churls, merciful; and dumb dogs, eloquent; your lazy drones, quick and nimble.'...

... No passion causeth greater alterations, or more vehement of joy or discontent. Plutarch, Sympos. Lib. 5. Quaest. I, saith, 'that the soul of a man in love is full of perfumes and sweet odours, and all manner of pleasing tones and tunes, insomuch that it is hard to say (as he adds) whether love do mortal men more harm than good.' It adds spirits and makes them, otherwise soft and silly, generous and courageous ...

... And if it were possible to have an army consist of lovers, such as love, or are beloved they would be extraordinary valiant and wise in their government, modesty would detain them from doing amiss, emulation incite them to do that which is good and honest, and a few of them would overcome a great company of others.'

Robert Burton, Love Improves the Lover,
from The Anatomy of Melancholy)

HINT! Search prose material for nuggets of speech-writing gold. If you don't have time to read out an entire passage like 'Love Improves the Lover' select a powerful line that summarises the observation you'd like to make. For example, you could quote Robert Burton as noting that love is a powerful force which ' makes wise men fools, so many times it makes fools become wise'.

Don't ignore longer pieces, they are filled with wisdom.

I wiped her nose! At her request
I rubbed and pinched with loving zest
That roguish feature numbed with cold,
As on the beach in Jan. we strolled
Mid icy blasts from north-nor'-west.
That it was red must be confessed,
And that I kissed it I'll attest,
And proudly shout to all: 'Behold!
I wiped her nose!'
She had no handkerchief–she guess'd–
I took out mine; softly caressed
That tender nose of fairest mould,
And kissed it, too! The tale is told.
On this my claim to fame must rest–
I wiped Her nose!

Eugene O'Neill, Rondeau, to Her Nose

The Owl and the Pussy-Cat went to sea
In a beautiful pea-green boat.
They took some honey, and plenty of money
Wrapped up in a five-pound note.
The Owl looked up to the stars above,
And sang to a small guitar,
'O lovely Pussy! O Pussy, my love,
What a beautiful Pussy you are,
You are,
You are!
What a beautiful Pussy you are!'

Pussy said to the Owl, 'You elegant fowl!
How charmingly sweet you sing!
O let us be married! Too long we have tarried:
But what shall we do for a ring?'
They sailed away, for a year and a day,
To the land where the Bong-Tree grows,
And there in a wood a Piggy-wig stood,
With a ring at the end of his nose,
His nose,
His nose!
With a ring at the end of his nose.

'Dear Pig, are you willing to sell for one shilling
Your ring?' Said the Piggy, 'I will.'
So they took it away, and were married next day
By the Turkey who lives on the hill.
They dined on mince, and slices of quince,
Which they ate with a runcible spoon;

And hand in hand, on the edge of the sand
They danced by the light of the moon,
The moon,
The moon,
They danced by the light of the moon.

Edward Lear, The Owl and The Pussy Cat

TIP!   Don't be afraid to be a little quirky.

To love 'very much' is to love poorly: one loves-that is all- it cannot be modified or completed without being nullified. It is a short word, but it contains all: it means the body, the soul, the life, the entire being. We feel it as we feel the warmth of the blood, we breathe it as we breathe the air, we carry it in ourselves as we carry our thoughts. Nothing more exists for us. It is not a word; it is an inexpressible state indicated by four letters ...

Guy de Maupassant, Our Hearts

Whate'er the theme, the Maiden sang
As if her song could have no ending;
I saw her singing at her work,
And o'er the sickle bending:
I listened, motionless and still:
And, as I mounted up the hill,
The music in my heart I bore,
Long after it was heard no more.

William Wordsworth, The Solitary Reaper

TIP!   While at first glance 'The Solitary Reaper' may just look like
        a poem about a man passing a woman, it symbolises an
        instant connection, so why not use to tell your bride or groom
        about the effect that they had on your heart the first time
        you met?

I wish I could remember that first day,
First hour, first moment of your meeting me,
If bright or dim the season, it might be
Summer or Winter for aught I can say;
So unrecorded did it slip away,
So blind was I to see and to foresee,
So dull to mark the budding of my tree
That would not blossom yet for many
a May.

If only I could recollect it such
A day of day! I let it come and go
As traceless as a thaw of bygone snow;

It seemed to mean so little, meant so much;
If only now I could recall that touch
First touch of hand in hand – did one
but know!

Christina Rossetti, Sonnet

———»·«———

Life has loveliness to sell,
All beautiful and splendid things,
Blue waves whitened on a cliff,
Soaring fire that sways and sings
And children's faces looking up
Holding wonder like a cup.

Life has loveliness to sell,
Music like a curve of gold,
Scent of pine trees in the rain,
Eyes that love you, arms that hold,
And for your spirit's still delight,
Holy thoughts that star the night.

Spend all you have for loveliness,
Buy it and never count the cost;
For one white singing hour of peace
Count many a year of strife well lost,
And for a breath of ecstasy
Give all you have been, or could be.

Sara Teasdale Barter

———»·«———

One hour to madness and joy! O furious! O confine me not!
(What is this that frees me so in storms? What do my
shouts amid lightnings and raging winds mean?)
O to drink the mystic deliria deeper than any other man!
O savage and tender achings! (I bequeath them to you my
children,
I tell them to you, for reasons, O bridegroom and bride.)
O to be yielded to you whoever you are, and you to be
yielded to me
        in defiance of the world!
O to return to Paradise! O bashful and feminine!
O to draw you to me, to plant on you for the first time the
lips of
        a determin'd man.
O the puzzle, the thrice-tied knot, the deep and dark pool,
all
        untied and illumin'd!
O to speed where there is space enough and air enough at
last!
To be absolv'd from previous ties and conventions, I from
mine and
        you from yours!
To find a new unthought-of nonchalance with the best of
Nature!
To have the gag remov'd from one's mouth!
To have the feeling to-day or any day I am sufficient as I
am.
O something unprov'd! something in a trance!
To escape utterly from others' anchors and holds!
To drive free! to love free! to dash reckless and dangerous!

To court destruction with taunts, with invitations!
To ascend, to leap to the heavens of the love indicated to me!
To rise thither with my inebriate soul!
To be lost if it must be so!
To feed the remainder of life with one hour of fulness and freedom!
With one brief hour of madness and joy.

Walt Whitman, One Hour to Madness and Joy

If you only knew how much I love you, how essential you are to my life, you would not dare to stay away for an instant, you would always remain by my side, your heart pressed close to my heart, your soul to my soul ...

... My Victor, forgive me all my extravagances. They are a further token of my love. Love me. I need your love as a touchstone of my existence. It is the sun which breathes life into me.

Juliette Douret to Victor Hugo (1833)

CHORUS:
Step it gaily, off we go
Heel for heel and toe for toe,
Arm in arm and off we go
All for Mairi's wedding.
Over hillways up and down
Myrtle green and bracken brown,
Past the sheiling through the town
All for sake of Mairi.

[CHORUS]

Plenty herring, plenty meal
Plenty peat to fill her creel,
Plenty bonny bairns as weel
That's the toast for Mairi.

[CHORUS]

Cheeks as bright as rowans are
Brighter far than any star,
Fairest o' them all by far
Is my darlin' Mairi.

[CHORUS]

Scottish Folk Song

9. THE CLASSICS

Let me not to the marriage of true minds
Admit impediments. Love is not love
Which alters when it alteration finds,
Or bends with the remover to remove.
O, no! it is an ever-fixed mark,
That looks on tempests and is never shaken;
It is the start to every wandering bark,
Whose worth's unknown, although his height be taken.
Love's not Times fool, though rosy lips and cheeks
Within his bending sickle's compass come;
Love alters not with his brief hours and weeks,
But bears it out even to the edge of doom.
If this be error, and upon me proved,
I never writ, nor no man ever loved.

William Shakespeare, Sonnet XLVI

TIP! Be dramatic! Shakespearean sonnets were written for orators with bravado and theatricality, so have some fun with them!

Shall I compare thee to a summer's day?
Thou art more lovely and more temperate:
Rough winds do shake the darling buds of May,
And summer's lease hath all too short a date:
Sometime too hot the eye of heaven shines,
And often is his gold complexion dimm'd;
And every fair from fair sometime declines,
BY change of nature's changing course untrimm'd;
But thy eternal summer shall not fade
Nor lose possession of that fair thou owest;
Nor shall Death brag thou wander'st in his shade,
When in eternal lines to time thou growest;
So long as men can breathe or eyes can see,
So long lives this and this gives life to thee.

William Shakespeare, Shall I Compare Thee To A
Summer's Day?

She walks in beauty, like the night
Of cloudless climes and starry skies,
And all that's best of dark and bright
Meet in her aspect and her eyes –
Thus mellowed to that tender light
Which Heaven to gaudy day denies.

One shade the more, one ray the less,
Had half impaired the nameless grace
Which waves in every raven tress,
Or softly lightens o'er her face,
Where thoughts serenely sweet express
How pure, how dear, their dwelling-place.

And on that cheek, and o'er that brow,
So soft, so calm, yet eloquent,
The smiles that win, the tints that glow,
But tell of days of goodness spent,
A mind at peace with all below,
A heart whose love is innocent.

Lord Byron, She Walks in Beauty

My Mistress' eyes are nothing like the sun;
Coral is far more red than her lips' red;
If snow be white, why then her breasts are dun;
If hairs be wires, black wires grow on her head.
I have seen roses damasked, red and white,
But no such roses see I in her cheeks;
And in some perfumes is there more delight
Than in the breath that from my mistress reeks.
I love to hear her speak, yet well I know
That music hath a far more pleasing sound;
I grant I never saw a goddess go;
My mistress, when she walks, treads on the ground:
And yet, by heaven, I think my love as rare
As any she belied with false compare.

William Shakespeare, Sonnet CXXX

In true marriage lies
Nor equal, nor unequal: each fulfils
Defect in each, and always thought in thought,
Purpose in purpose, will in will, they grow,
The single pure and perfect animal,
The two-celled heart beating, with one full stroke,
Life.

Alfred, Lord Tennyson (from The Princess)

FRIENDSHIP

... I have loved my friend as I do virtue, my soul, my God.
From hence methinks I do conceive how God loves men,
what happiness there is in the love of God.
... There are wonders in true affection:
... United souls are not satisfied with embraces, but desire to
be truly each other which being impossible, their desires are
infinite, and must proceed without a possibility of satisfaction.
Another misery there is in affection, that whom we truly love
like our own, we forget their looks, nor can our memory
retain the idea of their faces; and it is no wonder, for they are
our selves, and our affection makes their looks our own.

Sir Thomas Browne

10. ADVICE

If you observe a really happy man you will find him building a boat, writing a symphony, educating his son, growing double dahlias in his garden, or looking for dinosaur eggs in the Gobi desert. He will not be searching for happiness as if it were a collar button that has rolled under the radiator. He will not be striving for it as if it were a goal in itself, nor will he be seeking for it among the nebulous wastes of metaphysics. To find happiness we must seek for it in a focus outside ourselves.

W. Beran Wolfe

———

I am not one
Who must have everything; yet I must have
My dreams if I must live, for they are mine.
Wisdom is not one word and then another,
Till words are like dry leaves under a tree;
Wisdom is like a dawn that comes up slowly
Out of an unknown ocean.

Edwin Arlington Robinson (from Tristram*)*

I salute you. I am your friend and my love for you goes deep. There is nothing I can give you which you have not got; but there is much, very much, that, while I cannot give it, you can take.

No Heaven can come to us unless our hearts find rest in today. Take Heaven! No peace lies in the future which is not hidden in this present little instance. Take Peace! The gloom of the world is but a shadow. Behind it, yet within our reach, is Joy. There is radiance and glory in the darkness, could we but see—and to see we have only to look. I beseech you to look.

Life is so generous a giver, but we, judging its gifts by their covering, cast them away as ugly or heavy or hard. Remove the covering and you will find beneath it a living splendor, woven of love, by wisdom, with power.

Welcome it, grasp it, and you touch the Angel's hand that brings it to you. Everything we call a trial or a sorrow or a duty, believe me, that's Angel's hand is there; the fit is there, and the wonder of an overshadowing presence. Our joys too: be not content with them as toys. They too conceal diviner gifts.

Life is so full of meaning and purpose, so full of beauty—beneath its covering—that you will find earth but cloaks your heaven. Courage then to claim it, that is all! But courage you have, and the knowledge that we are pilgrims together, wending through unknown country, home.

And so, at this Christmas time, I greet you. Not quite as the world sends greetings, but with profound esteem and with the prayer that for you, now and forever, the day breaks and the shadows flee away.

Fra Giovanni, Letter to a Friend

I love you not for what you are, but I love you yet more for what you are going to be.

I love you not so much for your realities as for your ideals. I pray for your desires that they may be great, rather that for your satisfactions, which may be so hazardously little.

A satisfied flower is one whose petals are about to fall. The most beautiful rose is one hardly more than a bud wherein the pangs and ecstasies of desire are working for larger and finer growth.

Not always shall you be what you are now.

You are going forward toward something great. I am on the way with you and therefore I love you.
I Love You, Carl Sandburg

Carl Sandburg, I Love You

———⟫•⟪———

Let there be spaces in your togetherness. And let the winds of the heavens dance between you.

Love one another, but make not a bond of love; Let it rather be a moving sea between the shores of your souls.

Fill each other's cup but drink not from one cup.

Give one another of your bread but eat not from the same loaf.

Sing and dance together and be joyous, but let each one of you be alone, Even as the strings of a lute are alone though they quiver with the same music.

Give your hearts, but not into each other's keeping. For only the hand of Life can contain your hearts.

And stand together yet not too near together:

For the pillars of the temple stand apart, And the oak tree and cypress grow not in each other's shadow.

Kahlil Gibran, The Prophet

———❖———

To be glad of life because it gives you the chance to love
and to work and to play and to look up at the stars—
to be satisfied with your possessions but not contented with
yourself until you have made the best of them—
to despise nothing in the world except falsehood and
meanness, and to fear nothing except cowardice—
to be governed by your admirations rather than by your
disgusts—
to covet nothing that is your neighbor's except his kindness
of heart and gentleness of manners—
to think seldom of your enemies, often of your friends,
and every day of Christ; and to spend as much time as you

can, with body and with spirit, in God's out-of-doors—
these are little guide-posts on the footpath to peace.

Henry van Dyke, The Foot-Path to Peace

—————⇒•⇐—————

Loveliest of trees, the cherry now
Is hung with bloom along the bough,
And stands about the woodland ride
Wearing white for Eastertide.

Now, of my threescore years and ten,
Twenty will not come again,
And take from seventy springs a score,
It only leaves me fifty more.

And since to look at things in bloom
Fifty sprints are little room,
About the woodlands I will go
To see the cherry hung with the snow.

A.E. Housman, Loveliest of Trees, The Cherry Now

—————⇒•⇐—————

HINT! Metaphors are a great way to convey deep feelings. 'The
Loveliest of Trees, the Cherry Now' is not only about a
pretty cherry tree, but about making the most of your life —
appreciating beauty. There is a sense that you never have
enough time in a lifetime to truly get enough of beauty. This
is great advice for a wedding speechmaker to pass down
to the bridal couple.

'Now I order you as a penance to fix your every thought on love, night and day, without remission; think of it always, ceaselessly, bearing in mind that sweet moment whose joy is so long delayed And so that you may be a noble lover, I wish and command you to have your whole heart in a single place, so that it is not divided but quite entire, without deceit, since I have no liking for duplicity.... Take care not to lend it out, a wretched act in my eyes; but surrender it as an outright gift, and the greater merit will be yours ...

When you have given your heart as I have told you, there will be hard and cruel trials for you to undergo. Often, when your love comes to your mind, you will be forced to leave people's company so they may not see the trouble that racks you. You will keep yourself to yourself, sighing, lamenting, trembling and more besides, suffering in many ways: now hot, now cold, flushed one moment, pale another; no steady or recurring fever is so distressing. Before you escape you will have sampled all the pains of love.

He told me I would go in search of my beloved; and, if I found her, her beauty would kindle my passion all the more, though courage to address her would fail me, for only false lovers chatter freely. At night I would toss and turn, think she was in my arms, then, finding myself deceived. Lament aloud and pray for the dawn to come and end my misery. How, I asked, can lovers endure all these ills? The God answered that Hope would be my chief protector, while Fair Thought, Fair Speech and Fair Glance would also stand me in good stead. With that, he suddenly disappeared.

Guillaume de Lorris, Roman De La Rose

11. PHILOSOPHICAL

O while I live to be the ruler of life, not a slave,
To meet life as a powerful conqueror,
No fumes, no ennui, no more complaints or scornful
criticisms,
To these proud laws of the air, the water and the ground,
proving
   my interior soul impregnable,
And nothing exterior shall ever take command of me.
...O to have life henceforth a poem of new joys!
To dance, clap hands, exult, shout, skip, leap, roll on, float
on!
To be a sailor of the world bound for all ports,
A ship itself, (see indeed these sails I spread to the sun and
air,)
A swift and swelling ship full of rich words, full of joys.

Walt Whitman, A Song of Joys

Now what is love? I pray thee, tell.
It is that fountain and that well,
Where pleasure and repentance dwell.
It is perhaps that sauncing bell.
That tolls all in to heaven or hell:
And this is love, as I hear tell.

Yet what is love? I pray thee say.
It is a work on holy-day;
It is December matched with May;
When lusty bloods, in fresh array,
Hear ten months after of the play:
And this is love, as I hear say.

Yet what is love? I pray thee sayn.
It is a sunshine mixed with rain;
It is a tooth-ache, or like pain;
It is a game where none doth gain;
The lass saith no, and would full fain:
And this is love, as I hear sayn.

Yet what is love? I pray thee say,
It is a yea, it is a nay,
A pretty kind of sporting fray;
It is a thing will soon away;
Then takes the vantage while you may:
And this is love, as I hear say.

Yet what is love? I pray thee show.
A thing that creeps, it cannot go;

A prize that passeth to and fro;
A thing for one, a thing for mo;
And he that proves must find it so:
And this is love, sweet friend, I trow.

Sir Walter Raleigh, A Description of Love

—————◆—————

When we build, let us think that we build forever. Let it not be for the present delight nor for the present use alone. Let it be such work as our descendants will thank us for, and let us think, as we lay stone on stone, that a time is to come when those stones will be held sacred because our hands have touched them, and that men will say as they look upon the labor and wrought substance of them, 'See! This our Fathers did for us.'

John Ruskin, Builders

—————◆—————

TIP!   Use the 'Builders' citation as an analogy of marriage. When you enter into a union you're building something—not only for the present and for the two of you, but something much grander. You're bringing families together and paving the path for future generations. The message is to recognise the value and depth of the promises made at a wedding and cherish them always.

I follow Beauty; of her train am I;
Beauty whose voice is earth and sea and air;
Who serveth, and her hands for all things ply;
Who reigneth, and her throne is everywhere.

Sir William Watson, Epigram on Beauty

Time is
Too Slow for those who Wait,
Too Swift for those who Fear,
Too Long for those who Grieve,
Too Short for those who Rejoice;
But for those who Love, Time is eternity.

Henry van Dyke, Time Is

TIP! *Father of the Bride Tip!*

Make 'time' the theme or message of your speech and begin by saying that time has flown by very fast as you've watched your daughter grow up. Take the guests through a quick history of your daughter - from freckled kindergartener through to beautiful bride and end on this quote, summing it up.

Into the sunshine,
Full of the light,
Leaping and flashing
Morning and night.

Into the moonlight,
Whiter than snow,
Waving so flower-like
When the winds blow;

Into the starlight
Rushing in spray,
Happy at midnight
Happy by day;

Even in motion
Blithesome and cheery,
Still climbing heavenward,
Never aweary;
Glorious fountain,
Let my heart be
Fresh, changeful, constant,
Upward, like thee!

James Russell Lowell, The Fountain

HINT! Why not use the fountain as an analogy for the bride
—she's probably bubbling over with excitement and joy,
looking light and beautiful. Use your imagination ...

Beauty means this to one person, perhaps, and that to the other. And yet when any one of us has seen or heard or read that which to him is beautiful, he has known an emotion which is in every case the same in kind, if not in degree; an emotion precious and uplifting. A choirboy's voice, a ship in sail, an opening flower, a town at night, the song of the blackbird, a lovely poem, leaf shadows, a child's grace, the starry skies, a cathedral, apple trees in spring, a thorough-bred horse, sheep-bells on a hill, a rippling stream, a butterfly, the crescent moon—the thousand sights or sounds or words that evoke in us the thought of beauty—these are the drops of rain that keep the human spirit from death by drought. They are a stealing and a silent refreshment that we perhaps do not think about but which goes on all the time.

It is the smile on the earth's face, open to all, and needs but the eyes to see, the mood to understand.

John Galsworthy, Beauty

Give me a little less
with every dawn:
colour, a breath of wind,
the perfection of shadows,
till what I find, I find
because it's there.
Gold in the seams of my hands
and the desk light burning.

John Burnside, Prayer

All that I know
Of a certain star
Is, it can throw
(Like the angled spar)
Now a dart of red,
Now a dart of blue;
Till my friends have said
They would fain see, too,
My star that dartles the red and the blue!
Then it stops like a bird; like a flower,
hangs furled:
They must solace themselves with the
Saturn above it.
What matter to me if their star is a world?
Mine has opened its soul to me; therefore
I love it.

Robert Browning, My Star

———————

[She] is a man's best movable, a scion incorporate with his stock, bringing sweet fruit; one that to her husband is more than a friend, less than trouble; an equal with him in the yoke. Calamities and troubles she shares alike, nothing pleases her that doth not him. She is relative in all, and he without her but half himself. She is his absent hands, eyes, ears and mouth; his present and absent all...a husband without her is a misery to man's apparel: none but she hath an aged husband to whom she is both a staff and a chair.

Sir Thomas Overbury, A Good Wife

———————

The trees are in their autumn beauty,
The woodland paths are dry,
Under the October twilight the water
Mirrors a still sky;
Upon the brimming water among the stones
Are nine-and-fifty swans.

The nineteenth autumn has come upon me
Since I first made my count;
I saw, before I had well finished,
All suddenly mount
And scatter wheeling in great broken rights
Upon their clamorous wings.

I have looked upon those brilliant creatures,
And now my heart is sore.
All's changed since I, hearing at twilight,
The first time on this shore,
The bell-beat of their wings above my head,
Trod with a lighter tread.

Unwearied still, love by lover,
They paddle in the cold
Companionable streams or climb the air;
Their hearts have not grown old;
Passion or conquest, wander where they will,
Attend upon them still.

W.B. Yeats, The Wild Swans at Coole

Two roads diverged in a yellow wood,
And sorry I could not travel both
And be one traveler, long I stood
And looked down one as far as I could
To where it bent in the undergrowth;

Then took the other, as just as fair,
And having perhaps the better claim,
Because it was grassy and wanted wear;
Though as for that the passing there
Had worn them really about the same,

And both that morning equally lay
In leaves no step had trodden black.
Oh, I kept the first for another day!
Yet knowing how way leads on to way,
I doubted if I should ever come back.

I shall be telling this with a sigh
Somewhere ages and ages hence:
Two roads diverged in a wood, and I –
I took the one less traveled by,
And that has made all the difference.

Robert Frost, The Road Not Taken

Here
Is home.
Is peace.
Is quiet
Here
Is love
That sits by the hearth
And smiles into the fire,
As into a memory
Of happiness,
As into the eyes
Of quiet.

Here
Is faith
That can be silent.
It is not afraid of silence.
It knows happiness
Is a deep pool
Of quiet.
Here
Sadness, too,
Is quiet.
Is the earth's sadness
On autumn afternoons
When days grow short,
And the year grows old,
When frost is in the air,
And suddenly one notices

Time's hair
Has grown whiter.
Here?
Where is here?
But you understand.
In my heart
Within your heart
Is home.
Is peace.
Is quiet.

Eugene O'Neill to Carolina on her birthday,
Quiet Song in Time of Chaos

12. RELIGIOUS

Abide with me; fast falls the eventide;
the darkness deepens; Lord, with me abide.
When other helpers fail and comforts flee,
Help of the helpless, O abide with me.

2. Swift to its close ebbs out life's little day;
earth's joys grow dim; its glories pass away;
change and decay in all around I see;
O thou who changest not, abide with me.

3. I need thy presence every passing hour.
What but thy grace can foil the tempter's power?
Who, like thyself, my guide and stay can be?
Through cloud and sunshine, Lord, abide with me.

4. I fear no foe, with thee at hand to bless;
ills have no weight, and tears not bitterness.
Where is death's sting? Where, grave, thy victory?
I triumph still, if thou abide with me.

Henry F. Lyte, Abide with me

Oh perfect love, all human thought transcending
Lowly we kneel in prayer before thy throne (holy throne)
That theirs may be the love which knows no ending
Whom thou forever more doth join in one
Oh perfect love, we seek to ask thy blessing (bless us oh
Lord)
From this day forth you'll guide this union here (come and
abide)
Come and abide within this new beginning
As we in reverence seek your perfect will
Oh perfect love (perfect love), all human thought
transcending
Lowly we kneel in prayer before thy throne (holy throne)
That theirs may be the love which knows no ending
Whom thou forever more doth join in one

Dorothy Frances Gurney, O Perfect Love

For flowers that bloom about our feet;
For tender grass so fresh and sweet;
For song of bird and hum of bee;
For all things fair we hear and see,
Father in Heaven, we thank Thee!

Ralph Waldo Emerson, We Thank Thee

Love, like verdant spring,
Bright, beautiful thing,
    Steps forth from the winter of self;
Yet, like the fair dawn
On the poor man's lawn,
    Is too rich to be purchased by pelf.
Pure love, like the root,
Exists for the fruit,
    Content to lie hid from our view,
Beneath the cold sod:
The image of God,
    Who, pervading all things through and through,
Works ever the same,
Unheeding of blame
    Or praise–like the stillness of night–
In the untrodden waste,
And provinces vast
    And peopled concealed from all sight.
Pure love is the flower
That laughs when clouds lower,
    Expecting the soft vernal rains
To ripen the seed,
But takes little heed
    Of the ills her own beauty sustains:
Or like the fair star,
That shineth from far,
    When all things are buried in night;
But when the bright day,
With worthier ray,
    Robes nature in vesture of light,
So gently retires,

Till darkness requires
    Her aid, when she noiselessly steals,
Once more to her post
Of duty, and lost
    To all selfish interest, feels
The pure joy of love;
But soon as, above
    The sky verge, orbed Luna is seen,
She leaves night so fair,
As best, to her care,
    And retires to the blue depths serene.

Reverend J. A. Allen, Unselfish Love

Only the wise man draws from life, and from every stage of it, its true savour, because only he feels the beauty, the dignity, and the value of life. The flowers of youth may fade, but the summer, the autumn, and even the winter of human existence, have their majestic grandeur, which the wise man recognizes and glorifies. To see all things in God; to make of one's own life a journey towards the ideals; to live with gratitude, with devoutness, with gentleness and courage; - this was the splendid aim of Marcus Aurelius. And if you add to it the humility which kneels, and the charity which gives you have the whole wisdom of the children of God, the immortal joy which is the heritage of the true Christian.

Henry Frederic Amiel, Only the Wise Man

I

Let my voice ring out and over the earth,
Through all the grief and strife,
With a golden joy in a silver mirth:
Thank God for Life!

Let my voice swell out through the great abyss
To the azure dome above,
With a chord of faith in the harp of bliss:
Thank God for Love!

Let my voice thrill out beneath and above,
The whole world through
O my Love and Live, O my Life and Love,
Thank God for you!

II

As we rush, as we rush in the Train,
The trees and houses go wheeling back,
But the starry heavens above the plain
Come flying on our track.

All the beautiful stars of the sky,
The silver doves of the forest of Night,
Over the full earth swarm and fly,
Companions of our flight.

We will rush ever on without fear:
Let the goal be far, the flight be fleet!
For we carry the Heavens with us, Dear,
While the Earth slips from our feet!

James Thomson ('B.V.'), Two Lyrics

—————

Give up the world; give up self; finally, give up God.
Find god in rhododendrons and rocks,
passers-by, your cat.
Pare your beliefs, your absolutes.
Make it simple; make it clean.
No carry-on luggage allowed.
Examine all you have
with a loving and critical eye, then
throw away some more.
Repeat. Repeat.
Keep this and only this:
what your heart beats loudly for
what feels heavy and full in your gut.
There will only be one or two
things you will keep,
and they will fit lightly in your pocket.

Sheri Hostetler, Instructions

—————

Through love to light! Oh wonderful the way
That leads from darkness to the perfect day!
From darkness and from sorrow of the night
To morning that comes singing over the sea,
Through love to light! Through light, O God to thee,
Who are the love of love, the eternal light of light.

Richard Watson Gilder, Through Love to Light

Where the remote Bermudas ride,
In the ocean's bosom unespied,
From a small boat that rowed along,
The listening winds received this song:
'What should we do but sing His praise,
That led us through the watery maze
Unto an isle so long unknown
And yet far kinder than our own?
Where He the huge sea monsters wracks,
That lift the deep upon their backs;
He lands us on a grassy stage,
Safe from the storms, and prelate's rage.
He gave us this eternal spring
Which here enamels everything,
And sends the fowls to us in care,
On daily visits through the air;
He hands in shades the orange bright,
Like golden lamps in a green night,
And does in the pomegranates close
Jewels more rich than Ormus shows;
He makes the figs our mouths to meet,

And through the melons at our feet;
But apples plants of such a price,
No tree could ever bear them twice;
With cedars, chosen by His hand,
From Lebanon, He stores the land;
And makes the hollow seas, that roar,
Proclaim the ambergris on shore;
He cast (of which we rather boast)
The Gospel's pearl upon our coast,
And in these rocks for us did frame
A temple, where to sound His name.
O! let our voice His praise exalt,
Till it arrive at heaven's vault,
Which, thence (perhaps) rebounding, may
Echo beyond the Mexique Bay.'
Thus sung they in the English boat,
An holy and cheerful note;
And all the way, to guide their chime,
With falling oars they kept the time.

Andrew Marvell, Bermudas

O love that casts out fear,
O love that casts out sin,
tarry no more without,
but come and dwell within.
True sunlight of the soul,
surround us as we go;
so shall our way be safe,
our feet no straying know.
Great love of God, come in!
Well-spring of heavenly peace;
thou Living Water, come!
Spring up, and never cease.
Love of the living God,
of Father and of Son;
love of the Holy Ghost,
fill thou each needy one.

Horatius Bonar, O Love That Lasts Out Fear

13. FAMOUS LOVE LETTERS

Madam,

It is the hardest thing in the world to be in love and yet attend to business. As for me, all who speak to me find out, and I must lock myself up or other people will do it for me.

A gentleman asked me this morning, 'What news from Lisbon?' and I answered, 'She is exquisitely handsome.' Another desired to know when I had been last at Hampton Court. I replied, 'It will be on Tuesday come se'nnight. Prythee, allow me at least to kiss your hand before that day, that my mind may be in some composure. O love!-

'A thousand torments dwell about me!

Yet who would live to live without thee?'

Methinks I could write a volume to you; but all the language on earth would fail in saying how much and with what disinterested passion I am ever yours,

Sir Richard Steele to Mary Scurlock

My dearest Girl,

This moment I have set myself to copy some verses out fair. I cannot proceed with any degree of content. I must write you a line or two and see if that will assist in dismissing you from my Mind for ever so short a time. Upon my Soul I can think of nothing else. The time is passed when I had power to advise and warn you against the unpromising morning of my Life. My love has made me selfish.

I cannot exist without you. I am forgetful of everything but seeing you again—my Life seems to stop there—I see no further. You have absorb'd me. I have a sensation at the present moment as though I was dissolving. I should be exquisitely miserable without the hope of soon seeing you. I should be afraid to separate myself far from you ...

... I could be martyr'd for my Religion—Love is my religion—I could die for that. I could die for you. My creed is Love and you are its only tenet. You have ravish'd me away by a Power I cannot resist; and yet I could resist till I saw you; and even since I have seen you I have endeavoured often 'to reason against the reasons of my Love'. I can do that no more—the pain would be too great. My love is selfish. I cannot breathe without you.

Yours for ever,

John Keats to Fanny Brawne

———

All that you are, all that I owe to you, justifies my love, and nothing, not even you, would keep me from adoring you.

Marquis de Lafayette to Aglae De Hunolstein

———

I found you, as I thought, amiable, tender, & yet acute & gifted with no ordinary mind – one whom I cd look upon with pride as the partner of my life, who cd sympathise with all my projects and feelings, console me in the moments of depressing, share my hour of triumph, & work with me for our honour & happiness.

Benjamin Disraeli to Mary Anne Wyndham Lewis

I believe there is no holding converse, or carrying on correspondence with an amiable woman, much less a gloriously-amiable, fine woman, without some mixture of that delicious Passion, whose most devoted Slave I have, more than once, had the honour of being ...

... Take a little of the tender witchcraft of Love, and add it to the generous, the honourable sentiments of manly Friendship, and I know but one more delightful morsel, which few, few in any rank ever taste. Such a composition is like adding cream to strawberries: it not only gives the fruit a more elegant richness, but has a peculiar deliciousness of its own.

Robert Burns to Clarinda (Agnes MacLehose)

For your own honour I demand you to render me an account of myself. Am I not your property? Have you not taken possession of me? That you cannot deny, and I belong to you in spite of myself and of yourself, so let me at least deserve to be yours.

Jean Jacques Rousseau to Countess Sophie D'Houdetot

My dear Nora,

It has just struck me. I came in at half past eleven. Since then I have been sitting in an easy chair like a fool. I could do nothing. I hear nothing but your voice. I am like a fool hearing you call me 'Dear'. I offended two men today by leaving them coolly. I wanted to hear your voice, not theirs.

When I am with you I leave aside my contemptuous, suspicious nature. I wish I felt your head on my shoulder. I think I will go to bed.

James Joyce to Nora Barnacle

To be with the people one loves, says La Bruyere is enough – to dream you are speaking to them, not speaking to them, thinking of them, thinking of the most indifferent things, but by their side, nothing else matters. O mon amie, how true that is!

... However when every morning I wake up, I look for you, it seems to me that half of myself is missing, and that is too true. Twenty times during the day, I ask myself where you are; judge how strong the illusion is, and how cruel it is to see it vanish. When I go to bed, I do not fail to make room for you; I push myself quite close to the wall and lave a great empty space in my small bed. This movement is mechanical, these thoughts are involuntary. Ah! how one accustoms oneself to happiness.

Count Gabriel Honore de Mirabeau to Sophie de Mounier

Passion gives a strength above nature, we see it in mad people; and, not to flatter ourselves, ours is but a refined degree of madness. What can it be else to be lost to all things in the world but that single object that takes up one's fancy, to lose all the quiet and repose of one's life in hunting after it, when there is so little likelihood of every gaining it, and so many more probably accidents that will infallibly make us miss of it? And, which is more than all, 'tis being mastered by that which reason and religion teaches u to govern, and in that only gives us a pre-eminence above beasts. This, soberly consider'd, is enough to let us see our error, and consequently to persuade us to redeem it.

Dorothy Osborne to William Temple

———»·o·«———

Oh, now you are mine! At last you are mine! Soon – in a few months, perhaps, my angel will sleep in my arms, will awaken in my arms, will live there. All your thoughts at all moments, all your looks will be for me; all my thoughts, all my moments, all my looks, will be for you!

Victor Hugo to Adele Foucher

———»·o·«———

My heart glows with an affection for you at this instant so tender, so delicate, and so refined that I want words to express it.

I have a thousand things to say to you. I think, write, talk, work, love—all, all—only for you.

Benjamin Rush to Julia Rush

———»·o·«———

Good night. My door has not been opened once to-day, but what my heart palpitated. There were moments when I feared to hear your voice, and then I was disconsolate that it was not your voice.

So many contradictions, so many contrary movements are true, and can be explained in three words: I love you.

Julie De L'Espinasse to Hippolyte de Guibert

⟞⟐⟝

Love me. I need your love as a touchstone of my existence. It is the sun which breathes life into me.

Juliette Drouet to Victor Hugo

⟞⟐⟝

My heart overflows with emotion and joy! I do not know what heavenly languor, what infinite pleasure permeates it and burns me up. It is as if I had never loved!!! Tell me whence these uncanny disturbances spring, these inexpressible foretastes of delight, these divine tremors of love. Oh! All this can only spring from you, sister, angel, woman, Marie! ... All this can only be, is surely nothing less than a gentle ray streaming from your fiery soul, or else some secret poignant teardrop which you have long since left in my breast.

... Marie! Marie! Oh let me repeat that name a hundred times, a thousand times over; for three days now it has lived within me, oppressed me, set me afire. I am not writing to you, no, I am close beside you. I see you, I hear you ...Eternity in your arms ... Heaven, Hell, everything, all is within you, redoubled ... Oh! Leave me free to rave in my delirium. Drab, tame, constricting reality is no longer enough for me. We must live our lives to the full, loving and suffering to extremes! ... Oh! you believe me capable of self-sacrifice, chastity, temperance and piety, do you not? But let no more be said of this ... it is up to you to question, to draw conclusions, to save me as you see fit. Leave me free to rave in my delirium, since you can do nothing, nothing at all for me. Tis to be! to be!!!

Franz Liszt to Marie D'Agoult

———

Good night. My door has not been opened once to-day, but what my heart palpitated. There were moments when I feared to hear your voice, and then I was disconsolate that it was not your voice.

So many contradictions, so many contrary movements are true, and can be explained in three words: I love you.

Julie De L'Espinasse to Hippolyte de Guibert

———

My dearest Misser Pietro,
I know that the very expectation of something awaited is the greater part of satisfaction because the hope of possessing it lights up desire. The rarer it is, the more beautiful it seems, the commoner, the less so.

Lucrezia Borgia to Pietro Bemob

———

... my heart beats through my entire body and is conscious only of you. I belong to you; there is really no other way of expressing it, and that is not strong enough.

Franz Kafka to Felice Bauer

———

Passionate lovers would like the whole world to run according to their wishes.

Denis Diderot to Sophie Voland

⸺⟡⸺

Through snow and frost a flower gleams. As my love does through ice and the evil weather of life. Perhaps I shall come today. I am well and tranquil and I believe that I love you more than yesterday. But that belief grows with every single day.

Johann Wolfgang von Goethe to Charlotte Stein

⸺⟡⸺

Sweetest Fanny,

You fear, sometimes, I do not love you so much as you wish? My dear Girl I love you ever and ever and without reserve. The more I have known you the more have I lov'd. In every way – even my jealousies have been agonies of Love, in the hottest fit I ever had I would have died for you. I have vex'd you too much. But for Love! Can I help it? You are always new. The last of your kisses was ever the sweetest; the last smile the brightest; the last movement the gracefullest.

When you pass'd my window home yesterday, I was fill'd with as much admiration as if I had then seen you for the first time. You uttered a half complaint once that I only lov'd your beauty. Have I nothing else then to love in you but that? Do not I see a heart naturally furnish'd with wings imprison itself with me? No ill prospect has been able to turn your thoughts a moment from me. This perhaps should be as much a subject of sorrow as joy – but I will not talk of that. Even if you did not love me I could not help an entire devotion to you: how much more deeply then must I feel for you knowing that you love me.

My Mind has been the most discontented and restless one that ever was put into a body too small for it. I never felt my Mind repose upon anything with complete and undistracted enjoyment – upon no person but you. When you are in the room my thoughts never fly out of window: you always concentrate my whole senses. The anxiety shown about our Loves in your last note is an immense pleasure to me: however you must not offer such speculations to molest you any more: nor will I any more believe you can have the least pique against me.

John Keats to Fanny Brawne

———

TIP!   Longer pieces like love letters can be broken up into short, poignant quotes.

I was never so miserable at leaving you as tonight, not even that first time when I left you in New York ...

We have been so very much together these last ten days, and so wonderfully happy. In all our twelve years of marriage, I do not think there has been anything to equal it.

You grow always not only dearer to me but more necessary, and you become all the time better, wiser and more to be adored.

Duff Cooper to Diana Cooper

———

For all time is worse than lost that's spent where thou art not, thou only relish to all other pleasures. Tis you alone that sweetens life, and makes one wish the wings of time were clipt, which not only seems but really flies away too fast, much too fast, for those that love (shall I be vain and say) like us; for that instead of breeding a satiety in either, (you see I answer for you boldly,) the common fate of vulgar friendships, does but heighten the vehemence of our desires for a more intimate (if that be possible) and lasting enjoyment of each others conversation and love. Ah! my dear, how I could expatiate on this fruitful theme, were it not day-light already, which if thou knewest, I am sure, Pray, my dear, goe to bed, would be your request to, my dearest life, your faithful friend and constant lover, J Hervey.'

John Hervey, 1st Earl of Bristol, to Elizabeth Hervey

<hr/>

The soul, so superior to the body to which it is bound, would remain on earth in intolerable solitude, if it were not allowed to some extent to choose from among all the souls of other men a partner to share with it misery in this live and bliss in eternity. When two souls, which have sought each other for however long in the throng, have finally found each other, when they have seen that they are matched, are in sympathy and compatible, in a word, that they are alike, there is then established for ever between them a union, fiery and pure as they themselves are, a union which begins on earth and continues for ever in heaven. This union is love, true love, such as in truth very few men can conceive of, that love which is a religion, which deifies the loved one, whose life comes from devotion and passion, and for which the greatest sacrifices are the sweetest delights. This is the love which you inspire in me, which you are bound to feel one day for another, if, to my everlasting misfortune, you don not already feel it for me. Your soul is made to love with the purity and passion of angels; but perhaps it can only love another angel, in which case I must tremble with apprehension.

Victor Hugo to Adele Foucher

———————

... So if you are idly curious as to whether I am still in love with Stella, the answer is yes yes yes yes yes yes yes yes yes yes yes yes yes yes yes yes yes yes yes yes yes yes yes yes yes yes yes and a million times yes ...

Cannot help it. Am quite sensible, quite able, quite myself, and yet a lad playing with you on the mountains and unable to feel where you begin and I leave off. And if you tell me that you feel like that the sky will not be high enough for me (isn't that a nice Irish phrase?) Heavens! how delicious it is to make love to you!!!!!

George Bernanrd Shaw to 'Stella' (Beatrice Campbell)

———————

My darling Bill,

I want you to realise what a tremendous difference you make to my life. Days are so much happier because of the wonder of you and your love. Somehow I have felt it – inadequate – to take out a pad and write to you. What is there new to say? Each day, the wonder of love and joy is renewed when I realise that the world has you in it.

It is Sunday and the fire is blazing in a Christmassy way.

It reminds me of a night when we put out the light and sat by the fire. It was painful to be so close to you in those days ... but then so wonderful to discover that we felt the same about each other.

I didn't really love you in those days, like I do now ... I was still a kid and didn't know what it was to love so much that it tore at one's insides to see the door shutting on one's dream man.

It was not long before you taught me, not only love for you, but utter givingness to others. It radiates from you all the time.

It sounds as though I found it tough falling in love. It was so difficult not to. I suppose women don't usually blather like this to their men folk, but I can't bear your not knowing that you mean more to me than anything or anyone. More even than bananas! Rough seas and stormy skies, miles of land and water cannot cut us off from each other. One day, the bells will ring again and it will be my happiest day. I belong to you.

Helen Cook to Bill Cook

⸺⸱◦⸱⸺

Scott,

There's nothing in all the world I want but you—and your precious love. All the material things are nothing. I'd just hate to live a sordid, colorless existence—because you'd soon love me less and less and I'd do anything—anything—to keep your heart for my own. I don't want to live—I want to love first, and live incidentally. Why don't you feel that I'm waiting —I'll come to you, Lover, when you're ready. Don't—don't ever think of the things you can't give me—You've trusted me with the dearest heart of all—and it's so damn much more than anybody else in all the world has ever had. How can you think deliberately of life without me? If you should die—O Darling—darling Scott—It'd be like going blind. I know I would, too. I'd have no purpose in life—just a pretty—a decoration.

Don't you think I was made for you? I feel like you had me ordered—and I was delivered to you—to be worn—I want you to wear me, like a watch, charm or a button hole bouquet to the world. And then, when we're alone, I want to help—to know that you can't do anything without me.

Zelda Fitzgerald to F. Scott Fitzgerald

———➤◦◄———

TIP!   *Short quotes!*

You can break up love letters like the one from Zelda to Scott Fitzgerald to get short, sharp quotes.

'I want to love first and live incidentally.'

'You've trusted me with the dearest heart of all.'

'I feel like you had me ordered—and I was delivered to you—to be worn—I want you to wear me, like a watch—charm or a button hole bouquet—to the world.'

Though still in bed my thoughts go out to you, my Immortal Beloved, now and then joyfully, then sadly, waiting to learn whether or not fate will hear us. I can live only wholly with you or not at all—yes, I am resolved to wander so long away from you until I can fly to your arms and say that I am really at home, send my soul enwrapped in you into the land of spirits. Yes, unhappily it must be so—you will be the more resolved since you know my fidelity—to you, no one can ever again possess my heart—none—never—Oh, God! why is it necessary to part from one whom one so loves and yet my life in W. [Vienna] is now a wretched life—your love makes me at once the happiest and the unhappiest of men ...

Be calm, only by a calm consideration of our existence can we achieve our purpose to live together—be calm—love me—today—yesterday—what tearful longings for you—you—you my life—my all—farewell—Oh continue to love me—never misjudge the most faithful heart of your beloved L.

ever thine
ever mine
ever for each other.

Ludwig Van Beethoven to his 'Immortal Beloved'

Love, as I told you is a plant of tenderst growth: treat it well, take thought for it and it may grow strong and perfume your whole life. But treat it carelessly, leave it a whole week without a word and suddenly when you want it, you'll not find it.

Frank Harris to Rita (Erika Lorenz)

I think that never in a thousand letters could I ever begin to tell you what it means to me to be able to come home to you. I never realized how starved I was for this deep wonderful sweetness, a small place where my love lives which he gives to me as my own and tells me is mine.

It's a symbol of the sweetness and the peace I know with you.

It's made up of all our hours together – the hours of the days and nights we have had together. It means music to me, and the blessing of good food, preparing it for you and me to eat together. It means the talking one can only do with one's dearest, closest, oldest friend and the silence one falls into only with this friend. It means all the happy things done together, and work that suddenly became play because it has been shared with a friend and a lover.

Margaret Lawrence to Benedict Greene

14. SAMPLE SPEECHES AND SNIPPETS

FATHER OF THE BRIDE:

WHAT A LOVELY BRIDE!

'Ladies and gentlemen, I'd like to start by pointing out that I had a hand in the making of the vision of beauty you see before you (Pause). Sweetheart, you look stunning!'

'Andrea, you look absolutely radiant and I couldn't be more proud of you. Out of all of the dresses I've seen you wear through the years—including the impressive bright purple tutu you used to charge around in—this one is definitely my favourite.'

'Rebecca, you have to forgive me, until today I still saw you as my little girl, but now I see what a beautiful woman you have become and I am proud and honoured to have given you away today.'

MANY THANKS!

'... before I continue I'd like to offer special thanks to my brother Rob and his wife Suzie for sponsoring the flowers at today's wedding. I didn't even realise you had such good taste—they look amazing.'

'A big thank you goes out to Ron's parents, Verity and Ryan, for sponsoring the drinks, to Nanna Genevieve for preparing the table settings and to my lovely wife, Lauren, for keeping a cool head in the lead up to the wedding and looking so incredible tonight.'

'I'd like to extend a big thank you to Leontine, Sibell and Archie for taking three planes, two trains, 75 kilos of luggage and a crazy taxi ride to be here today. We're delighted that you could share this very special day with us.'

NEW SON

'... I clearly remember when Jess first brought Luke home. I had my shotgun ready. Or I would have had I owned one. Luckily it turned out that he's actually a lovely chap even though he supports The Dragons. He also seems to make Jess very happy and I've grown terribly fond of him myself. Welcome to the family, son. I'm glad I'll have some time to work on your sporting taste.'

'I don't know Moe very well, but I know my daughter, so I can deduct that he's patient, intelligent, adventurous...and

(Pause) ... tall. He also seems to cause Ailene to glow, which is impressive. I'm glad to have a magician in the family. I look forward to getting to know you better.'

WHEN SHE WAS SMALL...
'To the untrained eye Kate may look like the perfect picture of a lady, but for those who have seen her grow up, I can assure you that's not true. From the moment she could crawl, she preferred mud and puddles to dolls. She got through her teenage years playing sports and avoiding dresses. But, as it turns out it was for the best because somewhere between running around a soccer field and climbing mountains, she managed to meet Tim. Together they have explored the mud and puddles of the world and my wife and I couldn't be more proud of them.'

FATHER OF THE BRIDE SAMPLE SPEECH
Thank you (MC) for your kind words. I'll pay you later.

Ladies and gentlemen, when (BRIDE) was eight she asked me why people get married. In a moment of parenting genius I told her that it was because they fall in love and want to live happily ever after. She fell silent, cocked her head and said, 'It's about the dress, isn't it?'

Having looked at the preparations that have gone into this wedding I can say with all confidence that it is most certainly not only about the dress. And I'd like to take this opportunity to thank (NAMES OF PEOPLE WHO CONTRIBUTED TO THE PLANNING OR FUNDING OF THE WEDDING) for making the other non-dress parts look so very impressive.

I'd also like to extend my thanks to all of you for coming, especially (GUESTS) who came all the way from (PLACE).

Sweetheart, you look radiant and the dress does look beautiful. But today is about so much more than that. It's about beginning a new life together, about the promises you've made to each other and about bringing a new football fan into our family. (GROOM) we're thrilled to have you.

(BRIDE'S MOTHER) and I knew that you were something special when (BRIDE) came home one Saturday night with eyes sparkling and cheeks ablaze. The only other time she got that look was when, as a three year old, she'd manage to escape bath time and go running naked through the front yard.

Understandably we were perplexed when we saw the look return. Was it a relapse? Should we contact the neighbours? (Pause)

You can imagine our relief when we found out that the cause of the look was a pleasant-looking boy. (Pause) With all of his clothes on.

Three years have passed since that time and we've gotten to know and love (GROOM) and his parents. So, looking at the two of you today, with those same streaker smiles on your faces, fills us with incredible joy and pride. We want to wish you all the very best for your future together.

Before I finish, could I please have everyone upstanding to join me in a toast.

To the bride, to the groom and to the dress.

GROOM:

THANK YOU!

'Sarah and I want to thank you all for coming and sharing our special day. We'd also like to give you props for being the best looking wedding party in Sydney today. And we're not just saying that because you've showered us with amazing gifts.'

'Thank you all for coming and for the incredible gifts you've brought. We are absolutely blown away by your generosity.'

'I wanted to extend my greatest thanks to Sukham's family. Not only have you made me feel like a part of your family from our very first meeting, but I owe you a debt of gratitude for bringing up such an incredible daughter. You've done an incredible job and I am going to work very hard to deserve her.'

'Mum and Dad, this wedding could not have happened without you. You have been a force to be reckoned with, a chauffeur service when one was needed, a stress ball when things got tense, a sounding board when we came up with our plans and a stationery shop when they didn't quite work out. Thank you for all of the effort you've put into today.'

SWEET NOTHINGS FOR THE BRIDE

'Michelle, I want you to know that you look beautiful. Thank you for saying yes, I look forward to our future together.'

'I had a speech prepared but I'm finding it a little bit hard to focus because of the beauty by my side. Baby, you look stunning and I want you to know that if I mess up my speech, it's all your fault.'

'Laura, from the first moment I met you I knew that there was something special about you. Aside from how beautiful you are, you have the most generous heart, the best sense of humour and an uncanny ability to read my mind. I don't know how you do it, but now I have our whole life to find out. I love you. Thank you for saying yes.'

A REAL LOVE STORY

'I'm not sure if you're all familiar with how Stacie and I fell in love. She worked across the street. I noticed her one lunchtime when she ordered and devoured the biggest sandwich I had ever seen. It was amazing, I'd never seen such a thin girl so bravely fight the laws of physics. So I stalked the sandwich shop hoping that between giant bites she would notice me. It took her three weeks. We went out for dinner, she didn't eat me and the rest is history.'

ROMANTIC

'Anne, I wanted you to know how much you mean to me, so I found this poem:
Not from the whole wide world I chose thee,
Sweetheart, light of the land and the sea!
The wide, wide world could not inclose thee,
For thou art the whole wide world to me.

I want you to know that you're not only my world but my entire universe. I love you.'

GROOM SAMPLE SPEECH

Thank you (MC) for introducing me, although I hope everybody already knows who I am (that is the lucky man married to the most beautiful woman in the room).

And thank you (FATHER OF THE BRIDE) for your kind words. I feel very privileged to now be a part of your family.

On behalf of my wife and I, I'd also like to thank all of you for coming to share our special day. You're all very dear to us (Pause)... And it wouldn't be anywhere near as much fun if I was speaking to an empty room.

I'd also like to thank my parents not only for raising me to be worthy of my bride, but for all of the love and support they've given us throughout our relationship and especially in the lead-up to the wedding.

Thanks must also go out to my best man who has been at my side with a beer in hand whenever I've needed it and to the lovely bridesmaids for all of their incredible help.

Finally I'd like to thank my bride, not only for saying yes today but for making me the envy of every non-related red-blooded male in the world. You look absolutely stunning and I can't believe I'm lucky enough to be spending the rest of my life with you. (Pause)

... Although there was a time when I thought we would never get to this point. You see, (BRIDE) and I used to work together and it wasn't too far into our acquaintance that I worked out she was the kind of girl I wouldn't mind getting to know a little better. Unfortunately for me, she was completely oblivious to my insight and failed to notice my smooth pick-up moves.

I had to take up dance lessons with her just to put the idea in her head. It's a good thing that our personalities clicked because, as you'll get to see a little later, there is no way I could have wooed her with my dancing alone.

But our personalities did click and she finally realised what I had known all along—we are great together.

(TURN TO BRIDE) Going forward I promise to continue to look out for your best interests, take care of you and—if need be—take more dancing lessons.

Now I'd like to propose a toast.

To the beautiful bride.

BEST MAN

MANY THANKS!

'(GROOM), thanks for your kind words, but your schmoosing isn't going to change my speech ... and stop stuffing $50 bills down my pockets.'

CONGRATULATIONS

'Good evening, Ladies and Gentlemen. Let me start by saying that the bridesmaids look absolutely gorgeous today, and only rightly outshone by our bride, Phoebe. And, I'm sure you'll agree with me gentlemen, today is a sad day for single men, as another beauty leaves the available list. And ladies, I'm sure you'll agree that today passes by without much of a ripple.'

– *Michael Hanrahan*

CRICKET WISHES

'If you can all indulge me for a moment I would like to bestow upon Geoff and Sidonie a Cricket Blessing:

'May your marriage commence at 6 runs an over, may you be composed in both defence and attack, may you duck the bouncers and dig out the yorkers, may your days be filled with sunshine, fresh air and green fields, when you occasionally knick the ball may your families be there to catch you at wicketkeeper with your friends at first slip, may you chase down big scores and defend any small totals.

For Geoff, may Sidonie be your post match masseuse and for Sidonie may Geoff be Errol Allcott's magic spray. May the life you are commencing today together be your greatest partnership and when you are old and the Great Umpire in the sky is going to call Stumps may you look back on your lives together and say 'How good was that!'

– Simon Trowell

FIRST MEETING

'I've known Simon since we were both toothless and obsessed with crayons. His personality has been pretty much set from around that time. He is an intelligent, fun, caring person but he does have one major downfall—punctuality. If you organise to meet up with Simon, you can be almost certain that you will be reaching a point of homicidal frustration when he'll stroll in, look mildly surprised and say something like, 'I thought you said 1pm?' So I knew that he had met someone special when I went over to his place and found him in an uncharacteristic rush. He was meeting Maria two hours later. Around the corner from his house. This was serious.'

SO CHIC!

'Brian wasn't always as well-dressed as he is today. In fact Lisa probably picked out this suit. But the fashion faux pas that I remember most vividly is his 'bright stage'. When he was about sixteen, Brian discovered a passion for fluoro and then against his own better judgement and our advice incorporated it into every part of his wardrobe. He even got a round bright orange clip-on earring because he thought it would make him look cool (and he was too afraid to get his ears pierced). He'd walk around, reflecting light from miles around and nodding suggestively at girls. So frankly, I think it's a bit of a miracle that he managed to find someone as beautiful and fashion savvy as Lisa.'

BEST MAN SAMPLE SPEECH

Thank you, (MC), for the introduction and to (GROOM) for his attempt at bribing me with kindness. I appreciate the effort, but the people need to hear the truth about you. (TURN TO GUESTS) Intelligent, handsome, funny... but enough about me, I should probably tell you all about (GROOM).

We met at university when (GROOM) walked into a glass door and nearly knocked himself out. It was the funniest thing I had seen and I couldn't help laughing. I assumed that once he had regained his orientation (GROOM) would clock me in the head, but instead he joined in and the two of us stood laughing like idiots outside of the university library.

That's one of the great things about (GROOM)—his ability to laugh at himself. He is one of the most intelligent people I know and yet does some of the dumbest things.

But the one thing he got right is his choice in partner. (BRIDE) is not only beautiful, ambitious and intelligent, but just as capable at laughing at (GROOM) as he is. You can always tell when they're together because their laughter precedes them wherever they go. They seem to be able to joke their way through any situation. And I sincerely wish that they are able to laugh through everything together.

(GROOM), it has been a real honour to have been chosen as your best man and (BRIDE) a real pleasure to be a part of your special day.

Now—not that you need it—I'd like to wish you both the very best of luck and happiness in your future lives together.

Ladies and gentlemen, could you please raise your glasses. To the bride and groom.

MOTHER OF THE BRIDE:

THANK YOU!

'I just wanted to reiterate how very thankful my husband and I are that Chen and Dave have such an amazing circle of friends and family. Today has been a real testament to the kind of love and joy they surround themselves with and a truly happy, memorable day. So for that I'd like to thank you all.'

MOTHERS AND DAUGHTERS

'Girls and their mothers have a special relationship. It is unlike anything else in the world and I am truly thankful for having it in my life. From the moment I held Sahiba in my arms on the 15th of September, I knew that she was special. She looked into my eyes, smiled and then peed on me.

That set the theme for our relationship. Over time since she was born, we haven't always seen eye to eye, we've had our share of disagreements, but through it all we've always had an incredible bond. I love Sahiba very, very much and I cannot find the words to express the joy and pride that I feel looking at her today. Darling, you look radiant.'

WHEN SHE WAS LITTLE

'One thing that can be said for Tamara is that she has never been a shy character. When I took her for her first day at school I was expecting tears and pleas. I had prepared myself to be strong. We neared the schoolyard and walked past terrified, crying five-year olds and distressed mothers and I thought, 'Oh no, that's going to be me at any second.' Then

Tamara stopped, looked at me and said 'Okay mum, you can go.' She was ready for her new adventure to begin. That spirit and curiosity has stayed with her and it propels her to succeed. And, I'm sure, it will ensure that her marriage is always strong, exciting and bravely moving forward.'

NEW ADDITION

'Daniel, welcome to the family! I assume Tuesdays work for you for our weekly family visits?'

'Everyone has been complImenting Louise. And of course I agree that she looks stunning, but I think Paul is getting a bit of a sore deal because he is looking very handsome. So let me take the opportunity to say that I really like the suit that Louise picked out for you, Paul.'

'Nathan, I'm so pleased to say that you've gone from our unofficial to our official son. The smile on your face tells me that maybe you're not aware of what you married into, but don't worry, I'll be over all the time to remind you.'

'Stewart, welcome to our family. You've felt like a part of it for a long time, but I'm glad to see it's official now. I love you very much and am very thankful that you and Clara found each other. I wish you all of the happiness in the world.'

EXTENDED FAMILY

'The fantastic thing about today is that we've not only gained a new son, but some extended family as well. John's parents, Felipe and Carla, welcome into our family. Thank you for bringing up such a fantastic son. We love him as our own and look forward to getting to know you better.'

MOTHER OF THE BRIDE SAMPLE SPEECH

(MC), thank you for the introduction.

I know that it is not customary for mothers of the bride to speak, but how could I resist? My little girl is getting married and I have been there to embarrass her at every other major event, so why not her wedding as well?

(BRIDE) was born on an exceptionally stormy night. The midwives told me that according to folklore that meant that the baby would have a strong character. I laughed. And it was the last time for about three weeks. (BRIDE) had a character and a set of lungs that could rival Pavarotti.

Over the years she changed from stubborn baby, to stubborn teenager to driven youth to ambitious student to successful, inspiring woman. She completed her university studies, got a fantastic graduate position and just so that there were no mistakes about how well she was doing, she managed to meet a man who was just as accomplished, just as intelligent and just as kind as her.

Today I want to thank you all for being at the next landmark stage of (BRIDE'S) achievements—her marriage to her perfect match, (GROOM).

Her father and I couldn't be more proud of her achievements, her attitude in life, the beautiful woman that she has become or her choice of husband.

Honey, you have always filled our life with joy and exceeded all expectations. I want you to know that we are very, very proud of you and that you look amazing. Thank you for being such an incredible daughter.

(GROOM), welcome to the family. We love and think very highly of you. Thank you for coming into (BRIDE'S) life and sweeping her off her feet and also for introducing us to your parents, who I can already tell will be good friends of ours in no time.

With all of that said, there's not much left other than to wish you every success in your future lives, but I can already tell by the way you two look at each other that your marriage will be filled with love, energy and happiness.

So there's just one thing left to do.

Ladies and gentlemen, could you please charge your glasses to the bride and groom.

BRIDE:

FREEDOM OF SPEECH

'I've been told that a good wife can cook to perfection, iron with her eyes closed and shouldn't speak at her wedding, so I'd like to take this opportunity to apologise to my husband and also to say, "Ha ha, you're stuck with me."'

'I know that brides don't traditionally speak at weddings, but I just have too much to say.'

MR RIGHT

'I really don't know how I did it, but I've managed to find someone who is in sync with what I'm thinking and yet manages to surprise me every single day. Sweetie, you're a comforting force that keeps me on my toes. Like magic.'

'Baby, I just wanted to say that I feel incredibly privileged not only to know you but to have you as my husband. T. Tolis famously said, 'To love is nothing. To be loved is something. To love, and be loved, is everything.' And you are and create my everything. I can't wait for our future!'

THANK YOU!

'I have so many thankyous to give that I won't be surprised if music starts playing and someone ushers me away from the microphone, but so many people have had a part to play in making today happen. Thank you to my parents— both original and gained by marriage—your support has been invaluable. Thank you to all of you for coming today, you have made this event really special. Thank you to our handsome groomsmen and lovely bridesmaids for dealing with the tantrums, posing for the photos and taking charge of flowers. Finally, thank you to my husband. You are everything to me and I'm so happy to finally be your wife. I love you. Cue the music.'

WE ARE FAMILY

'To Edward's family, thank you for accepting me and welcoming me into your lives with such ease. Any nerves that I might have felt when first meeting you disappeared within seconds. And now I can't imagine my life without you. You are not only Edward's parents, but have become my close friends. I'm thrilled to officially be a part of you.'

LOVE AT FIRST SIGHT

'James and I met at a party—he was dressed as a pirate, I was dressed as a pirate; it was meant to be. Pirate love. But I actually didn't realise he was my soul mate until some weeks later when he laughed with me over burnt toast. There was really nothing funny about it, just black toast, but that was a really defining moment. Because I think in life, it's the little things that end up making the biggest difference and from that moment, I knew that we could laugh our way through anything.'

POPPING THE QUESTION

'I'm not sure whether everybody is familiar with our proposal story, so I thought I'd embarrass Oliver a little by retelling it. We went on a trip to Vietnam. What I didn't know was that Oliver had been planning to pop the question for weeks and now the opportunity was in sight. Only he wanted it to be so good that the time never seemed right. Then on our second-last night there, with the help of a little Dutch courage, slightly swaying from side to side he finally managed to slur out the words, 'I have a pretty ring for you'. How could I resist?

BRIDE SAMPLE SPEECH

Thank you (MC) for my glorious introduction and thank you to my husband for making my life.

I know that (GROOM) has already thanked everybody, but I'd like to reiterate just how much it means to us to have you all here celebrating this day with us. You've all been such a big part of our lives it's an honour to have you watch us take our next big step.

I'd also like to send out a quick thanks to the catering team, our function coordinator, the band and the photographer who have all been doing an amazing job.

My biggest gratitude, however, is destined for my and (GROOM's) parents who have been supportive, understanding and completely unphased by some of the wedding dramas we've encountered. I don't know how we would have done without you.

And, of course, thank you to my new husband. I love you more than I know how to express. You are my life and you've completely transformed my life. In the words of Robert Browning:

I would that you were all to me,
You that are just so much, no more—
Nor yours, nor mine—nor slave nor free!
Where does the fault lie? what the core

Of the wound, since wound must be?
I would I could adopt your will,
See with your eyes, and set my heart
Beating by yours, and drink my fill
At your soul's springs—your part, my part
In life, for good and ill.

I love you! Let's grow old together.

Now I'd like to propose a toast to all of you who have made our day so very special.

To our honoured wedding guests.

MAID OF HONOUR:

MANY THANKS!

'Ursula, thank you for picking me to be your maid-of-honour. It has been a huge honour and a real pleasure to stand by your side through one of the biggest events of your life and it is a memory that will stay with me.'

LIFE AS A SHOE

'Since (BRIDE) loves shoes, I'd like to bestow a little shoe blessing on the happy couple: May your marriage be as glorious as a Jimmy Choos store, may you have both style and comfort, may you avoid blisters and unstable ground, may your days be filled with smooth surfaces, sunshine and glamour. When you occasionally chip off your heel or lose a shoelace may your family and friends be there with spares, may you chase the big sales but notice the small department stores. For (GROOM) may (BRIDE) be your heel-grip and for (BRIDE) may (GROOM) be your water protector. May the life you are commencing today together be your greatest ensemble and when you are old and your heels finally snap, may you look back on your lives together and smile.'

ANGEL

'The one thing that has always amazed me about Beth is her selfless nature. This is a girl who would gladly sacrifice her own comfort if it meant easing someone else's. And she would do it without a second thought. But although she is generous, she is not weak. She will always spring to the defence of her friends and stand up for what she believes is right, and those qualities are so rare in a person that for every day of our twenty-year friendship I expect her to reveal her wings and instead every day she has remained constant in my life and brought comfort and love to it. Ben, you are a very lucky man, not everybody gets to marry an angel.'

ADVENTURES

'One of my favourite memories of Leah is when, as mischievous teenagers, we decided to truant and go for a road trip in a northerly direction. The plans were spontaneous—made on our way to school so we drove without a map. And before you knew it we got stuck in a thunderstorm in some tiny town in northern Victoria with a flat battery. My mind went into panic mode—my parents couldn't find out that I hadn't gone to school, they would skin me, but Leah remained calm, put her hand on my arm and said, 'Don't worry, it's not the end of the world. It'll be alright.' And it was.

Since that time we've gone through bigger things, but something that has always stayed with me is an admiration of a person who can at once be passionate and spontaneous and on the other keep a perspective on life. They are incredible qualities and she is an incredible person.'

PARTNER IN CRIME

'You know, Shakti, I wouldn't give my best friend up to just any bloke who walked in and swept her off her feet. But as I've gotten to know you, I've noted a really kind heart, a quirky sense of humour, and an ability to plan for the future without forgetting to live in the present. All of those things make you perfect for my best friend. You have my blessing, you may now kiss the bride. Wait? Have we done this part already?

MAID OF HONOUR SAMPLE SPEECH

What a great introduction! Thanks (MC).

Thanks also go out to the previous speakers, because at least one of them gave us, the bridesmaids, a compliment and with the bride looking so radiant, I'm impressed they even looked our way.

(BRIDE), you look stunning and everything that a bride should be. I know that I feel a little short of breath just looking at you, so I'm not sure how (GROOM) is managing to breathe, but he hasn't passed out yet, so we'll take that as a good sign.

Before I get into the mischief we've gotten into together, I just wanted to thank you for giving me the opportunity to be your maid of honour. I'm really touched and honoured to have been so involved with a day that is so important to you.

I also wanted to say a quick thanks to the rest of the bridal party, who did such a wonderful job walking down the aisle, posing for photos and helping me fight my nerves.

I'm actually not even sure why I am so nervous, when the star of the show, (BRIDE), is so very clearly calm. It must be the effect of love because when I first met her she was thumping her legs and arms into the ground and screaming uncontrollably. (Pause) To be fair, she was four at the time. (Pause)

When the pre-school teacher managed to calm her down a little and asked her why she was so upset, she simply stated that one of the boys in the class didn't want to play with her.

I'm glad that she's refined her pick-up technique (a little bit) since those days. Although (GROOM) is so kind hearted that had he seen her in a tizzy of flailing arms he probably would have walked over and played with her. Some things are just meant to be. And you two, you are definitely meant for each other. I hope that you, (BRIDE), keep your calm demeanour and that if you ever feel the need to stomp, that you, (GROOM), will be there to comfort her and provide her with friendship. I think you two are going to have a blast in your new life together.

And on that note, I'd like to propose a toast.

Could everyone please charge their glasses to (BRIDE) and (GROOM'S) married life.